DEDICATION

To the two females that changed my life:
my wife Carla, the most caring person I know,
and Sabrina, a four-legged child that I will never forget.
This book is for you.

TABLE OF *contents*

Introduction

I don't know about you, but I grew up listening to, and then watching, Rin Tin Tin, Lassie and Sergeant Preston of the Yukon with his loyal dog King.

It was a time when radios and then television sets, came in beautiful mahogany cabinets, and were the family gathering place in the evening and on weekends. Sound and picture quality left something to be desired, but listeners and viewers made up for this lack of quality with their imagination.

As a boy growing up, I dreamed of owning a big dog, a dog that was smart, loyal and responded to my every command.

We lived in a four-flat during the 1940's, and although pets were allowed, the rooms were too small for anything larger than a poodle.

One day, my dream of a big dog came true for twenty-four hours. A friend of my father decided he had to find a home for their young boxer. Dad liked dogs, so this became his chance, as well as mine, to have a big dog. He scooped up Freda, that was her name, drove home and managed to bring her into the house before my mom got home from work. You can probably guess the rest.

"Take her back, she's huge, and besides, we don't have the room," my mom declared. "Give her a chance, the kids will love her. She's very gentle," dad responded.

With both of my parents working at the time, the only pets allowed in our house were a goldfish and a parakeet named Tweetie.

In an effort to defend our new addition, dad convinced mom to allow Freda to stay for a day in order to prove her good manners. Next morning, two large chairs were strategically placed in order to confine her to a single room and keep her out of mischief.

Several hours later, Freda greeted my mother at the front door. She was gone the next morning, ending a childhood dream.

I graduated college in 1959 and trust me, a dog was the last thing on my mind. It was time to join my friends and begin our chase for new and larger dreams. The years that followed produced a slew of material things and throwaways, which, looking back, were really one in the same. If something was new, I had to have it. The latest cars, the longest and best vacations, a new home, a second home — even a third!

I've had more than my share of toys as my ability to earn escalated, including one of the first Jaguar XKE's. Just as with my dreams of one day having a big dog, I never forgot the first time I saw an XKE parked next to a hotel in Chicago. I was just a kid at the time, but I remember saying to myself, "one day I'll own one of those." Who knew? In 1984, I bought one and later had it rebuilt for playtime.

My love of sailing began with a small sailboat, a Snipe. It was given to me when I was twenty. Here again, as the years passed, my boats grew in size.

No deposit — numerous returns. That was the nice thing about collecting things. You could always replace them with something newer, bigger or better, on a whim!

Growing up, I was constantly drawing pictures of cars. As an adult, I had the good fortune to live my childhood dream by participating in the design and build of them.

I traveled the world and earned enough money to retire early to a waterfront home in Florida, confident that if I was careful in my later years, I wouldn't find myself greeting folks as they entered the local Wal-Mart.

It wasn't until I had done my part to ruin two marriages that I realized I lacked feeling and that caring trumped being a workaholic. My wife Carla taught me to love.

A house filled with cats, taught me to feel, and a dog named Sabrina, taught me the importance of prayer and the fact that God watches over all of us. We just don't realize it!

On October 27, 2006 I found myself sitting on the floor crying uncontrollably and wondering where the years had gone. I may have found myself but I had lost a loyal friend!

God Works in Mysterious Ways

Sitting on the floor in our vet's office the afternoon of October 27, 2006, I wished that I could turn back the clock. We had been blessed to have Sabrina with us far longer than we ever imagined, and yet, it seemed like only yesterday that she had come into my life.

She taught me to care. Taught me to love and taught me the importance of believing.

I was never overly religious growing up. Sure, I believed in God, but I found that I could get along just fine without him, or at least I thought I could. I was wrong!

What brought on this awakening? First, my wife Carla. Next, a houseful of cats and finally, a very special dog.

Funny thing about pets, some people treat them as disposable objects.

Now, before you disagree, hear me out.

During hurricanes and other natural disasters, what family member is most likely to be left behind? Not a wife or children. However, once the car is loaded with people, clothing, important papers and other family necessities, some pet owners have been known to leave the family pet behind — there just wasn't enough room in the car!

News stories have been written about owners that killed their pets before evacuating. Other stories talk about owners that chained or tied their pets to the nearest tree, left to die, or turned them loose to fend for themselves. If their pets were lucky enough to be found by first responders or by the Humane Society, they were held for a period of time. If they were not claimed, they were put to sleep.

This is not one of those stories. It is a story about lessons learned the result of several kittens and cats, and a dog that came into my life and turned it upside down.

I will never forget the first time I saw and held Sabrina. She was nine and a half weeks old and weighed twenty-four pounds, twice the normal weight of a puppy her age. She was a round and fuzzy ball of fur, that looked more like a baby bear than a German shepherd, but her head, already long, her coloring, and her eyes gave her away. As she looked up at me, I found myself thinking "'*til death.*" It was love at first sight!

During our nearly eleven years together, Sabrina's veterinary bills would have caused many owners to question her importance. Cheaper to turn her out, give her away, or drop her off at the pound and let them dispose of her. After all, she was just a dog.

I know what professional trainers tell us — "they're just dogs." Not to me. Never! She was a member of our family and we were fortunate to have her. During that time, I came to understand the meaning of the words "'*til death.*" I believed that I did. Yet, I fail to understand why it took me so long to appreciate the meaning.

Maybe it was because during our time together, Sabrina, Carla and I traveled thousands of miles to see veterinary specialists. Hours were spent sitting, pacing and waiting by the phone for good news from her surgeons.

With each day that passed, my love for her grew stronger. She endured so much pain, so much rehabilitation. A lifetime of medications and yet, she did it with an ever present smile and an unbelievable disposition.

Time after time, I asked God to transfer Sabrina's pain to me — asked him to watch over her and to guide the hands of her caring surgeons as she lay motionless on the operating table.

Was this God's way of testing the lifetime commitment he created when he brought the two of us together?

It doesn't matter whether they are seven pounds or seventy. I've seen these four-legged "gifts" bring giants of industry to their knees and turn the allegedly cold-hearted to jelly with their antics.

October 27, 2006 is a date that will remain etched in my memory forever. As I sat on the floor with Sabrina, her head resting in my lap, my body shook. I knew what was about to happen, I'd been there before with our cats. I knew I was doing the right thing, but that didn't stop my tears, as a love that can only exist when it is deep and genuine, was about to be taken from me.

God had granted us nearly eleven years with Sabrina — far more time than her doctors thought we could expect based upon her health. Yet, at the moment when she was about to go to sleep for the last time, I wanted more!

I had promised myself that I would never allow her to live in pain needlessly. I would keep that promise no matter how much I hurt inside.

I learned more about myself in eleven years with Sabrina, than I had in my first fifty-seven.

If love is "a fleeting thing" then the unconditional love we shared was a gift from God for taking good care of his child. I cannot imagine anyone that has experienced the love of a pet, discarding it. Walking away and feeling nothing! Ours is a story about experiencing love, finding God and becoming a better person than I thought I could be.

"Unconditional Love" is dedicated to every dog and cat lover that has ever lost a special friend.

God knows who we are.

We have shared his special gift, a gift that can never be taken away from us — memories!

Cats! Have We Got Cats!

Like all stories, this one has a beginning — unusual by most standards — a heart — pounding middle, and a heartbreaking ending. And although I begin with my retirement, as you will soon find out, the story actually began thirteen years earlier.

Like most of us that have to work for a living, I dreamed of the life of a retiree. Leastwise, that's what I always thought before I retired.

As far as pets were concerned, they were just fine for someone else, but not me. My life revolved around my career. I didn't have time to sit around whispering soft words or showering love and affection upon a furry friend that didn't understand a word I was saying.

Prior to giving up the rat race, I dreamt of staying up late once I retired and getting up in the morning whenever I pleased. That dream didn't include getting up to feed the cats or take Sparky for a walk in a blizzard or rainstorm at six in the morning.

Just the thought of not having to race to the airport and then make a mad dash to catch a plane should have been enough to brighten my day.

I honestly believed that my calling it quits would mark the end of late night and weekend calls about one alleged emergency or another somewhere in the free world — problems that had to be addressed right now!

Never again would I feel guilty about sleeping in or just lounging in bed, reading the paper or a good book without having to watch the clock, or worry about unfinished projects at work.

So, as you can see, these thoughts were enough to bring tears of joy to my eyes as I settled into retirement.

Then it happened. My dreams went up in smoke. Here I am, fourteen years after retirement from the automotive industry and the corporate world, and the lights in our cattery still come on about six in the morning. Granted, that was later than my normal wakeup call. Most days, my morning began around five o'clock in order to make the drive to the office or the airport. As president and chief operating officer of a multi-divisional company, I had this insane idea that when I was in town, I had to be the first person to arrive at the office. And when I traveled, I had to make the most of the day by arranging the earliest possible flights in order to arrive at my destination while there was still time to get in a few hours of work.

Mine, was a dream job according to most of the people I met. Hardly a flight went by that didn't see the passenger next to me asking what I did for a living. When I answered, nine out of ten times, the response was the same, "wow, what a job!"

Frankly, those passengers were right. I was living my boyhood dream. Talk about being a kid in a candy store — that was me. But sooner or later age catches up with us, and that dream becomes a tedious reality.

My travels, when I was on the road, took me coast to coast. When trips to England, Europe, Mexico, South America and Southeast Asia were added to my itinerary, well, some people would call that exciting. Frankly, spending in excess of twenty-four hours on airplanes in order to get to a meeting, when you didn't sleep well on airplanes, wasn't my idea of "glamour."

Shortly after I retired to my life of leisure I was asked to consult for a group in Indonesia. I knew and liked the people and I was promised that their project would require no more than twenty-five hours a month, and infrequent travel to the west coast and Jakarta for meetings. The price was right and the task was interesting, so, how could I refuse?

Well, the task lasted six years. The hours piled up and as for the meetings, well, they went from one or two, to several meetings on the west coast and five or six, ten day to two week trips a year to Indonesia. I guess I was still a glutton for punishment. Thank goodness our cat breeding and show days were over.

If you are wondering about a cattery, well, think of it as a hotel for spoiled and pampered cats. Ours consisted of specially designed double-decked cages. Each cat had his/her own private apartment. The cats also had a play-yard built in the hotel common area consisting of multiple levels for jumping and scratching posts for additional exercise. I can hardly remember a time when we didn't have ten or more kittens and cats romping around the house.

Now, I know this may sound strange to all of you, but it isn't, not if you are a cat breeder that competes for international honors in the Cat Fanciers Association show program. It's the cat version of the American Kennel Club competition program for dogs.

Each year hundreds of cat breeders travel to weekend shows in order to display their best kittens and cats. These local shows, held from coast-to-coast, enable feline competitors to accumulate points sufficient to win an invitation to a national show at the end of each season. The better your kittens and cats do in regional and national competition, the more valuable your future litters become. I can't tell you how many kittens saw their first light in Carla's hands, or how often I was able to watch the miracle of birth. However, when it came time to offer our latest little tikes for sale to other breeders interested in improving the lines of their breed stock, saying goodbye to each child was a test of our will.

I worked during the week prior to retiring, and when I was home, we would pack our bags and fly, or load up the car and drive to shows on Fridays, usually returning home late Sunday, or early Monday morning so that I could repeat this weekly routine. On those weekends when I was away on business, Carla would head off to a show on her own, either by car or plane.

Work, in conjunction with this wacky schedule, should have made retirement a snap. After all, during my working career, rising early and working late was a way of life. Now that our remaining cats were retired from the show circuit, six o'clock should have seemed like the middle of the morning — but it didn't!

Why, God!

What makes this story different? I never wanted a cat or a dog. So, allow me to begin BC, before cats. Actually, make that, before a house full of cats, and after one lonely kitten, which by the way, was anything but a planned adoption.

I came into possession of said cat, quite by accident. Little did I know that at some point in the future I would meet my wife and find myself surrounded by furry felines.

When I was growing up we never really had a dog and I'm sure the thought of owning a cat never occurred to my parents.

Once I was on my own, if I thought about owning a pet — which I didn't — I'm sure I would have concluded that it would be little more than a time consuming distraction. That is, until my secretary left a shoebox on my desk one morning containing a black-and-white fur ball that just happened to purr and look like a kitten. I guess this was her way of telling me that we could both use some company.

I'd gone out to the west coast to attempt the turn-around of a company in chapter eleven, bankruptcy. I was up to my ass in alligators, working long days and even longer nights, so a cat wasn't on my top-ten list of things to acquire.

Company, who needs it? When you're a workaholic you don't have time for distractions.

Looking back, and truth be told, there's something about puppies and kittens guaranteed to melt the coldest hearts.

Now I'm not saying I was cold hearted, but a pet lover? Not really, at least not then. As far as I was concerned I didn't have time for one, leastwise, not until I lifted that kitten out of the shoebox and placed it on my lap. Too late, she had me in her paws!

Squeaks, as she became known, was my constant companion at the end of a long day. Her greeting was always the same. I'd sit down, and she'd jump into my lap, curl up, and begin to purr, or squeak rather than meow.

There was almost nothing special about Squeaks. She was a Heinz fifty-seven cat, if you know what I mean, with one exception, she wasn't aloof. I guess when you begin life in a shoebox and then find yourself being delivered to a stranger, you do everything possible to insure the fact that you've seen the last of shoeboxes.

As time passed I did come to find that Squeaks was, well, almost unique.

To the best of my knowledge, cats aren't big fans of water. They drink it, and that's where their curiosity ends.

As far as I know, most of these rather independent creatures aren't known for following behind their master, matching him step for step, much less stroke for stroke, in a swimming pool.

Cats aren't big on togetherness, and they definitely aren't known to be Olympic swimmers. Right? Wrong.

Having been a swimmer in high school and college, I've always made sure I had access to a pool. I made it a point to get up early when the weather warmed up, looking forward to a few laps in the pool before heading to the office.

One day I made the mistake of leaving one of the sliding doors to the pool area open as I headed for my morning exercise.

I walked out onto the pool deck with Squeaks following close on my heels. I didn't think twice about it. After all, that's where I could usually find her. Besides, the entire yard was enclosed, so where could she go?

I dropped my towel on a chaise. Squeaks made herself comfortable on the chair as I proceeded to dive in.

I cut the surface smoothly, enjoying the coolness of the water as it surrounded my body. As I began to stroke across the pool I turned my head for air and saw something I'll never forget. There was Squeaks, paddling along next to me. I almost drowned laughing.

Squeaks and I got along just fine for a few years. Then, I met my wife to be, and before long, we were married. Suddenly, I had a wife, and Squeaks had an entire family of exotic feline friends.

Well, they weren't exactly friends. Carla's pack of pampered show cats tolerated my "plain Jane" for a while, and then it was "odd cat out."

Apparently, pedigreed cats think rather highly of themselves. After much hissing, spitting and an occasional brawl, it became clear that we'd have to find a new home for Squeaks, which we did. She went to live with a very wealthy lady, and as best we were able to learn over the years, Squeaks was treated royally.

As for me, I, remained up to my eyeballs in cats. I won't attempt to remember all their names over the years, but to give you an idea of the size of our family, there was: Wolfe, Rachel, Charlie Brown, Schroeder, Jessica, Randy, Tony, Indy, Lucy, Peppermint Patty, Perrin, Ginger, and Muffy, to name just a few.

We not only had cats, we had kittens as well — lots of kittens. At times there were a dozen frisky felines romping around our house.

Over the years together I have to admit, I've come to enjoy the cats. I guess it is because no two are exactly the same.

We bred Oriental shorthairs. Some, we kept for breeding and show purposes. Others, we sold. According to my wife, Oriental shorthairs were a manmade breed. Because of that, they entered the world in an almost endless array of colors: solids, tabbies, bi-colors, and smokes. Every litter held a new surprise!

In case you haven't heard this before, you can train a dog. Cats are free thinkers.

Unlike dogs, most cats aren't constantly demanding affection. In fact, some cat owners will tell you that this lack of a "love me instinct" can be their most irritating trait. And, when you think about it, it makes sense. I mean, why have a pet if you can't find it to hug, rub and pet gently?

Cats are *not* dogs. You don't put them on a leash and go for long walks, you simply sit back and observe their "life without a care" attitude.

Deep down you hope that every now and again, if you call their name and they're not sleeping or too busy doing something important, they'll pay attention and eventually see fit to come forward to find out why you're bothering them.

Don't expect results when you reprimand a cat; it is not going to happen. In fact, you'll be lucky if they're still standing in front of you seconds after you begin your speech and finger pointing.

Cats have no shame. Either that or they think they're above reproach and never wrong. I'm not sure which!

One good reason for having a cat, if you must have a pet, they're self-cleaning. This means no late night walks in the rain or a snowstorm while you wait for them to take care of business.

Just feed them a couple times a day, keep their litter box reasonably clean, make water available, and you can move them around the world without ever expecting to hear a complaint.

If you're looking for a pet to serve as a watch person, take cats off your list. They'll be the first to surrender if an intruder comes into their home, that is, if he can find out where they're hiding.

I will never forget the time our house in California was robbed, while we were away at a cat show. We had driven to Phoenix for a show. When we arrived, after midnight, and walked up to the check-in desk, we were told to return home immediately. A neighbor had noticed our front door open and one of our cats walking back and forth, from the house to the front step. Knowing that our cats were never allowed outside, and finding us gone, she had called the police. The drive back at one in the morning was the longest trip I have ever taken, as Carla and I constantly switched off driving, all the while, wondering what we would find when we got home. Toward the end of our drive, we were switching off every fifteen minutes in order to stay awake.

When we walked into the house, we found that it had been ransacked and several valuables had been stolen. The thieves had left wrappers from their meal on our bed and strewn on the floor. Apparently, they had been watching the house for some time and knew that we were gone for more than a few hours.

Valuables are important, but our primary concern was the cats. How many had walked out the open door and were gone forever? We should have known better. Our cowards, a.k.a cats, afraid of any strange noise, had all gone into hiding and didn't come out until we arrived back home and began calling their names. One by one, they made their appearance.

As for the valuables, well, the robbers weren't too bright. They were caught, when one of them tried to pawn Carla's high school graduation ring. She had added it to the list at the last minute, never thinking anyone would try to sell it. Talk about luck. In the end, we got most everything back, and the thieves went to prison.

You can't expect much quality time with a cat. Toss a ball of yarn, as you would a ball with a dog and don't expect them to bring it back. They may bat it around for a while. But return it? Forget about it!

It's the little things that intrigue a cat!

Wad up a piece of paper and throw it on the floor and a cat will spend an entire afternoon batting it around the house like a hockey puck.

Although round the clock affection isn't a part of a cat's job description, Carla and I have enjoyed the company of more than a few members of our feline family over the years. That's right, some of them were actually happy to plant themselves on our chest or settle in on our lap and stay there until we moved.

Ironwolfe and Tony were like that.

Ironwolfe, affectionately known as "Mr. Wolfe" or just "Wolfie," was an ebony Oriental shorthair that, when stretched out, measured over thirty-six inches. He was "the Don" of the family, a star if you will, and he knew it.

"Wolfie," had been on TV several times, and during his life, enjoyed a show career filled with many fans and admirers. If cats came with egos, I'm sure 'Wolfie" had a big one.

"Mr. Wolfe" was also a social drinker. Not a drunk, mind you, not in the strict sense of the word. Yet looking back on our boy, he was the only cat I ever met that drank strawberry daiquiris with gusto.

My guess is that he liked the whipped cream on top and, when he got to the drink, found the sweetness of it to be equally appealing.

On the infrequent occasion when my wife and I would sit down to toast an event, we either made a drink for "Wolfie," or he got up in our face, stuck his long nose into our drink and joined the party. One way or another, he refused to be left out or ignored. Bottoms up!

Years later my wife informed me that she knew I was the right man when, during the dating process, Rachel, a lilac point Siamese, bonded with me. It seems Rachel was a good judge of male character and didn't cozy up to most males. Paws up and you were invited back. Paws down and you were out the door.

Tony was the only non-Oriental in our house. From the moment I saw an Ocicat at a show, I wanted one. They were a man's cat.

Compared to the Orientals we bred, Tony could best be described as my middle linebacker. He was a squared up block of muscle and an absolute love.

From the moment he arrived from a breeder friend in Amarillo, Texas, my chest became his favorite resting spot. It didn't matter if I was reading, talking on the phone, or just taking a cat-nap, I had to make room for "the boy" as he was affectionately known.

He'd plant himself on my chest and immediately begin to lick my face and nose. Next came a soft paw to the side of my head. If that didn't get the desired attention, he'd back up a few paces, put his head down, come forward and head butt me. This would continue until I stopped whatever I was doing and both talked to and stroked him.

As we'd look at each other, eye to eye, I often thought that as he grew older, if I put a pair of granny glasses on the end of his nose, he'd have made a great Sir Winston Churchill.

Because of a tumor found in his nasal passage when he was a year old, surgery had left him with a lifetime breathing problem. This, in a way, added to his Sir Winston mystique. Often, instead of breathing normally, he would harrumph. Although I was amused, I'm sure he didn't feel the same way.

Tony was also one of the few cats that would come on command if he wasn't already under foot.

When I was home, he'd move from room to room waiting for an opportunity to settle in on my chest. That was my "big" boy.

When you're a serious breeder, which my wife was, and you have more than a few felines living with you, which we did, your life is turned upside down. Life as you've known it takes on a whole new dimension fraught with decisions.

What second car do you buy? After all, it has to have room to carry the cats you're showing, their show tents and cages, toys, food, water, litter, and of course two humans and their luggage.

What do you do with twelve cats when you want to take a vacation?

You don't, unless you're fortunate to find a pet sitter in the neighborhood. Boarding all of them would have cost more than the vacation.

Finding a new house was no simple task?

I'll never forget our move from LA to Dallas. I remember stopping at one motel in particular. It had a sign out front that read, "No pets." It was late, so we checked in anyway.

When we got to our room we found it had a carpeted wall behind the bed.

We left some of the cats out of their cages while we went to dinner, and when we came back to the room, those that weren't climbing the walls and leaping to the bed, were sitting in the window waving to us. So much for secrecy!

Even house hunting took on an entirely different reality.

When your family consists of as many cats and kittens as we had at one time or another, you no longer set out to buy a house — you spend days, weeks and sometimes months searching for the *purrfect* cat-friendly environment, with room, of course, for humans.

First and foremost, the house has to have a room large enough for a cattery, a place where the children can play, poop, and sleep at night.

Over the years, I can't begin to count the number of houses that failed to pass the cat test. Not because there was anything wrong with the house, mind you, simply because it didn't have a large enough room for the kids.

I recall one instance where I offered to give up the master bedroom in order to buy a particular house on the beach, only to be turned down.

Another time, we actually built a room addition for the troops. Although we loved the house, no room was deemed to be satisfactory long term.

The construction task turned out to be a nightmare, but in the end the children were happy campers, and that's all that mattered.

Charlie B and Me

Sometimes — maybe once in your life — magic happens! As for me, well, I've been blessed, I just didn't realize it until I wrote this story. You see, it has happened to me at least three times that stand out in my mind. Carla was the first. Then along came Charlie Brown. Not the cartoon character, although that is who he was named after.

This Charlie Brown was a beautiful chestnut Oriental Shorthair kitten. During all the years we bred and showed kittens and cats, Charlie was the first, of only two kittens, that I adopted at birth. From the moment of birth, I declared, "he was mine!"

There's something special about a chestnut Oriental that's hard to explain. You have to see one to appreciate what I'm saying. Imagine a kitten with a warm, rich, dark chocolate coat and emerald green eyes that speak to you the moment you see him.

As to a name, well, it was pre-ordained. Carla and I didn't have to create lists and cull them down. Not this time. Instantly, he became Charlie Brown. As for the rest of his new brothers and sisters, well, they took on the names of characters in the strip.

Within weeks of birth, a vet found that Charlie had a heart murmur. At the time, he told us not to worry, that he'd be fine, he said, "Enjoy him, and allow him to live a normal life." So, that's what we did.

I thought Charlie was magnificent and could hardly wait until he was four months old and I was able to bring him out as a "kitten" and show him off on the show circuit.

With each new child you decide to "bring out" you dream of endless wins, admiring fans, a house filled with ribbons and trophies, and of course, the well deserved stardom, admiration, or scorn of your competitors.

Someone once wrote that, "beauty is in the eyes of the beholder." As much as I hate to admit it, they were right — at least this time.

During his first four months on the show circuit, entered in the "kitten" class, Charlie failed to attract the attention of a single judge. In fact, one judge picked him up, looked him over and declared, with enthusiasm I might add, "This, is an excellent example of a Havana Brown!"

Talk about insults. Thank goodness Charlie didn't understand English. As for me, I was angry. Competitors and show attendees were laughing at the two of us as I went up to his judging cage, picked him up and attempted to disappear, and then re-appear, back at our show cages. Why didn't they see what I saw!

Well, so be it. The two of us would head back to our show cages, sit down and drown our sorrows in carrot cake. You see, Charlie turned out to be very special in another way. From the first time I brought a piece of carrot cake back to our cage area during lunch, he had to have some. I don't know whether it was the cake or the creamy icing that he liked, but from that first taste, I had to make sure that when I had a piece of cake, so did he. Spare the rod and spoil the child!

At his last kitten show, a final for shorthair cats, before Charlie moved on to the "adult class" at eight months of age, he actually made a final. Paul Raines was the judge and he seemed to have liked Charlie in the early going, so we stayed to see if his number was put up for a final. When the numbers went up, we didn't see his number so we packed up and went back to the hotel. Charlie's kitten season ended as it had begun, without a single ribbon.

The next morning, when we returned to the showhall a friend and fellow breeder told us that Charlie had made his first final, in Paul's ring. We were heartbroken. How could we have left? She told us that when we weren't there, Paul made it clear that he would not award the ribbon or points to anyone.

Four months of teasing and ridicule from breeders, about my son, a.k.a "the ugly duckling," had passed and although we had nothing to show for our efforts, Charlie's father, that's me, wasn't about to give up.

I found Paul Raines and pleaded my, or rather, Charlie's case. After all, I was defending my child, right?

Paul finally relented and agreed to give me the rosette — 5th Best Shorthair Kitten. However, he made it clear that the points that went with it were lost forever. Points, be damned. It was the ribbon that mattered!

Four months had passed and to our fellow competitors, Charlie was a frog trapped in a kitten's body. "He was too this, and too that." The two of us downed a lot of carrot cake during those first four months, as we licked our wounds. Little did the nay-sayers know that before long, there would be a new "man" in town. That's right, before their very eyes, my little frog was about to grow up — and turn into a handsome prince!

Being a glutton for punishment, and highly competitive, I decided to show Charlie as a neutered adult, having reached the eight month age requirement.

Miracle of miracles, Charlie's body had suddenly begun to change and he began winning show after show. Not just any ribbons — this time he was walking off with first and second place honors.

Chances are the carrot cake had nothing to do with his new found success, but I kept it coming anyway.

It's not unusual for breeders to celebrate birthdays and the special designations that their favorite cats attain as they compete in shows.

Birthday and award cakes of all sizes and shapes were baked or purchased by their breeders, to mark these occasions. At times it seemed that each cake was bigger than the last, and all were large enough to provide slices for most if not all the exhibitors.

Charlie's dad, that's me again, promised, well, I actually boasted, that Charlie would have, "the biggest and best cake of all when he achieved his Grand Premiership," which as it turned out, he achieved very quickly.

So, in keeping with my promise, I searched and found the "Beverly Hills cake baker to the Stars," and ordered up a multi-tiered carrot cake confection, with a life size replica of Charlie Brown, the cat, of course, sitting proudly on top — with all the Peanuts characters romping around on the various layers.

As it turned out, Charlie's cake was so tall that we had a difficult time fitting it in the back of the car and protecting it from damage. However, we did just that and managed to get it to the show in one piece.

When it was time to unveil the cake and celebrate, you can guess who was first to the icing, that's right, Charlie. He dove in nose first.

In a matter of months, Charlie began piling up points. That's right, from no points as a kitten, my little guy was within five points of winning the CFA Southwestern Region in his class, Grand Premiership. Not bad for an ugly duckling!

Because we were off to one show after another on weekends, breeders call it "campaigning," Monday morning was not my favorite day. That is, until, in order to keep me off the highways late at night and insure the fact that I would be home at a respectable hour in order to get a good night's sleep, Charlie was offered use of our company plane. To this day, Charlie may well be the only cat that had his own twin engine, pressurized Aerostar, complete with Captain, at his disposal.

Keith was his pilot. He later went on to fly for American Airlines. But during that hectic show season, Charlie could be found sitting majestically in the right seat, keeping an eye on the instruments and directing traffic, as the two of them delivered Carla and I to one show after another.

Charlie turned out to be the highest scoring show cat in the history of our cattery. Sadly, he didn't have time to enjoy his wins or his new found fame and an unbelievable number of fans. There would be no life of leisure, with just the two of us, sitting around eating carrot cake in retirement.

I wrote a story toward the end of the season that appeared in the Cat Fanciers magazine titled, "Charlie B, and me," recounting our time together.

Charlie Brown died in his second year. You see, the heart murmur that we'd been warned about when he was a kitten, finally caught up with him.

I was away on a business trip when Carla called to tell me that Charlie had not been acting himself. She was at the vets and was confronted with a major decision, Charlie needed heart surgery — now. She wanted to know whether to allow the vet to try and save him. I told her to do everything she could.

Well, "everything," wasn't good enough. Charlie died that day, and although it was his heart that ended his life, that little guy had a heart that was many times larger than his small body. More important, he had captured my heart. This was the first time I cried and demanded that God tell me, "how could he take one of his own — so young!"

I wrote another story that appeared in Cat Fanciers magazine titled, "Charlie Brown — he won me." He may have been dead, but he would never be forgotten.

Charlie campaigned the same way he attacked carrot cake, straight ahead and full of enthusiasm. He loved having people swoon over him and judges show him off. He lapped up every bit of adulation that came his way.

We'll never know if the strain of traveling from show to show caused his little heart to give out.

Charlie was gone, but I had a scrapbook full of memories!

We had four chestnut oriental kittens during sixteen years of breeding. Charlie was our first and he would be our last. The other males were sold to breeders. The female was sold as a pet because of white on her coat. There would never be another Charlie Brown!

Years later, Scrappy, that's what we called him, came in to the world too weak to stand. He was such a little guy, just like Charlie, but he came to us with the same warrior's heart.

We knew almost immediately that he had a problem — you sense these things after a while — so we wrapped him up, kept him warm and talked to our vet. He told us we could either put him down or try to build up his little legs. We chose life!

First, we would place him on the floor and one of us would lie down with him and try to coax him forward, while the other was within reach of him. I don't know why or how, but that little guy would struggle and move his body with every ounce of strength that he had — and he would come to us. I guess that's why we called him Scrappy — he never gave up!

When we weren't working with him on the floor, we would fill our bathtub with warm water, Carla would be inches away, in order to keep him from going under, while at the other end of the tub, I would coax and cheer him on as he tried to paddle his way to me. He never stopped trying.

Scrappy put up one hell of a fight for over a week before his little heart gave out. Like Charlie, he fought to survive.

We only kept two chestnut Orientals during years of breeding. Both left us, far too early. But, both made quite an impression.

Lokey, the Stranger at Our Door

The Nashville area doesn't handle cold and snow very well. It takes about a quarter of an inch of snow to declare a national disaster. Stores are emptied of all food staples. Most drivers, already a menace, turn into pilots as they stomp on the gas pedal in order to get up a hill, then fly off into never never land and oncoming traffic on the other side!

Snow isn't a regular occurrence in Nashville, so I was more than a bit surprised when I returned from a business trip to find it cold — about ten below, and snowy — several inches of the white stuff.

I thought the annual winter ice storms in Dallas were something to write home about, but this day was only going to get better. I'd just returned from meetings in Melbourne, Florida — part of the consulting contract I had entered into when I retired and I wasn't exactly dressed for the abrupt change in the weather.

Well, here I was, making my way down the very steep hill that led to our house, ever so slowly. The county didn't clear our road even though we were inside the county boundaries. Their response to our pleas: "It is a private road, do it yourself." Frankly, I thought they just wanted to avoid making the three-mile trip out of town to get to the five of us that lived in the boonies, down on the Cumberland River.

I inched my way down our road, making sure to avoid a very steep drop on one side of the car. Suddenly, a very large, gold-colored dog that didn't belong to me came running up the road to escort me down to our carport. With my survival instincts working overtime, I crept down the snow-covered hill with the car in low gear. I didn't want to drop over the hill and into my neighbor Steve's front door — and I didn't want to hit the dog.

Once I reached the bottom of the road, I stopped short of our carport. Fido had now positioned himself in the center of it and seemed to be protecting his turf. I waited, and he stood his ground. He wasn't moving from the entrance, so I decided to chance opening my car door. Fido continued to stand his ground. He wasn't growling, so carefully, I got out of the car and immediately found myself being greeted like a long-lost relative. This four-legged monster was all tongue and tail wags.

Now, keep this picture in mind. This wasn't just a dog; this was a very big dog, probably well over one hundred pounds. However, being brave and not sure I could outrun him in a foot race to the front door, I took a chance, closed the car door and stood still, all the while hoping that this greeting wasn't an attempt on his part to lull me into a false state of security.

Some people believe that if a dog's tail is wagging that's a good sign. So, as his tail wagged, I ran my hands back and forth over his rather large head. Surprise of surprises, when I stopped, my hands were still attached to my arms.

Next, I massaged his ears, all the while speaking words of praise that I knew he didn't understand. He seemed to be overly friendly for such a big guy. While we were in the process of bonding, my wife exited the front door to see what all the commotion was about.

I continued to inspect Fido and concluded that he was a cross between a German shepherd, a Labrador retriever, and an elephant.

"What do ya think?" my wife called out.

"Think? Who's had time to think? I've been too busy trying to hold Godzilla off without offending him and becoming his next meal. Where'd he come from?"

"Come inside. It's quite a story. Don't worry. He won't bite you if you move," she responded, "he's a real love." So, I left my newfound friend, who by the way was big enough to saddle, standing outside the front door with his tail now in overdrive.

Once inside the door, I took a closer look at the carport, and noted that a bed had been set up in a protected corner, along with water and food bowls. Obviously we had a guest. Were we about to add a new member to the family?

This, I was sure, would not be considered a good sign if you were one of the eight show cats I knew had gone into hiding at the first sound of barking.

Knowing their reaction to anything out of the ordinary, I was positive the only thing saving our guest from the pound was the fact that the cats didn't know how to dial 911.

"So who's the new boarder?" I asked — never really believing "it" was here to stay.

"Beats me," Carla responded. "He just showed up in the yard a few days ago."

"I was outside shoveling snow, and for some reason I felt as though someone was watching me. I looked up, and there was this large golden dog looking at me."

That, in and of itself, was a minor miracle, as finding our doorstep was no simple task even in good weather — unless you knew exactly where you were going.

When we went house hunting for a retirement home in the greater Nashville area several years earlier, the realtor needed a compass, an area map, a couple of phone calls, some very detailed instructions and breadcrumbs in order to locate this fixer-upper and then find his way back to civilization.

Our house was well back in the woods, on the banks of the Cumberland River, a good three miles from a small town east of Nashville called Gallatin.

The house was far enough from civilization to know that in the event of a fire, the volunteer fire fighters didn't stand a snowball's chance in hell of reaching us in time to avoid a total loss.

When my city-dwelling sister and brother-in-law came from Florida, to visit us, they suffered immediate culture shock. Their first question was, "How can you live out here in the middle of nowhere? Where are the malls, the shopping centers?"

My response to how we lived could be summed up in a word, "Quietly."

As for major shopping, we were several miles away from shopping centers, malls and traffic, and frankly, we loved every minute of it.

Our road, if you want to call it that, was a not very well-marked gravel affair. It was little more than a turn off a backwoods, two-lane highway, identifiable by a ram-shackled old farmhouse. Miss the barn and the road ended in two miles.

At first blush, you would think that would have made it easy to find us, but you'd be wrong. Most of the farmhouses in the area looked like throwbacks to the Civil War.

I'm painting this picture so that you can better understand how difficult it had to be for Fido to navigate his way to our doorstep. Without a handheld GPS and hundreds of dog treats strewn along the ground to lead his way through the forest or along our private road, he didn't stand a chance. We were over a mile from traffic, what little there was, with woods and farmland on one side of us and the river on the other.

"I couldn't turn him away. The last several days have been brutally cold. He's just a puppy," my wife said.

"A puppy, what'll he be when he grows up?" I responded. "And how do you know he's just a puppy? Look at the size of him."

"I opened his mouth and checked his teeth," she said.

"You what! Look at that head. Are you crazy. You could've been eaten alive," all the while forgetting that my wife had been around dogs and cats her entire life.

"His teeth are very white. That's a pretty good sign that he can't be more than a year old, if that," she pointed out.

How comforting, I thought. As far as I was concerned, checking his teeth was tantamount to placing your head in a lion's mouth and asking if he wanted something to eat.

Well, we talked some and then some more and determined that either he'd gotten loose and strayed from home or had been dumped along the side of the road, in the snow and cold — left there to die by a heartless owner.

Either way, by some miracle — or hand of fate if you're not an optimist, which in this case I preferred to be — he'd managed to find his way to the one home God knew wouldn't turn a cold and hungry traveler away.

Carla told me that after several attempts to chase him off, followed by repeated attempts to ignore him, she'd surrendered.

As you might expect, all we had in the house for pets was cat food, so she fed him a can of that and made him a bed outside in the carport where he'd be out of the wind.

He was so hungry that after eating birdseed that had dropped from our feeders, he probably thought the cat food was a meal fit for a king.

"The weather continued to be rotten, and when he didn't leave the next morning I walked up the road to our neighbor Joe's house," Carla explained.

They had a cocker spaniel, so she knew he would have some dog food that she could borrow.

Obviously, no good deed goes unrewarded. Our four-legged hobo adopted Carla. She said that for the past few days she couldn't walk around outside or walk the quarter-mile to get the mail without Junior attached to her hip, and this without a leash.

Thinking about it, I decided having him around might not be a bad thing. He was big, and if he didn't wag his tail, he'd obviously scare the hell out of most mere mortals, to say nothing of uninvited guests.

Prior to leaving on my first business trip, I'd called the local sheriff and asked if he'd have a car check the house periodically while I was gone. Small town living does have its advantages. Knowing where we lived, he agreed to send a car by several times a day and again at night. He told me to call him whenever I was going to be gone.

Try getting that response in the big city!

Getting back to the problem at hand, what to do with Fido, Carla and I came to the same conclusion. "We can't keep him," we said in unison.

We agreed that we needed to try and find his owners and let them know he was safe and in good hands. This, of course, assuming he'd simply strayed from home — an overly optimistic assumption on our part under the circumstances.

Besides, we agreed, even if we could keep him — which we knew we couldn't — once the cats got a look at him they'd lose eight of their nine lives on the way to safety on top of their sleeping cages.

Neither one of us was big on having pets and keeping them outside. As far as we were concerned they were family and needed to be treated that way — inside the house!

So over the next few weeks we called every vet and shelter in the area to see if anyone had reported the loss of a dog matching Lokey's description.

We put up posters, left descriptions in several vet offices and ran ads in local newspapers that reached most of the surrounding towns.

Everyone has to have someone that loves them, so why not our guest?

Don't ask me how or why we came up with the name Lokey. We probably should have named him No Key, for leaving home without one, but that implied that he wasn't too bright, which turned out to be far from the truth.

After weeks of trying to find his owner, and with nothing to show for our efforts, Lokey was still a resident in our carport. No one had stepped up to claim him.

Having determined that we'd done everything we could, we concluded that either he was about to become the newest member of our four-legged family or we had to find a good home for him.

The decision was a difficult one. We were beginning to fall in love with the big lug, he was a real love and stuck to us like glue wherever we went. I guess he didn't want to give up a good thing, having apparently missed more than a few meals before arriving on our doorstep.

My wife had grown up around golden retrievers and Labradors and although she was a cat lover, she had a special place in her heart for big dogs.

I'd never had one for more than a day and made it a point to tread carefully around dogs, especially the ones that looked like they might enjoy having me for lunch.

Besides, over time I'd become fond of cats. Deep down I knew that dogs and cats weren't known for swapping Christmas cards or inviting one another to Thanksgiving dinner.

The solution, though painful, was as clear as the nose on your face. It was time to run a new series of ads in the local papers with hopes of finding Lokey a loving family.

Having assumed the role of canine matchmaker, we could only hope that our selection of a family would suit both parties.

Being a large dog and clearly stating this fact in our ads seemed to narrow the field where adoption was concerned. For a while it looked like we'd never find a home for him other than ours.

To our surprise, the ads didn't stop more than a few small dog lovers from coming out to take a look. Having done so, we weren't shocked when, upon seeing Lokey's size, they said, "Thanks, but no thanks," as they beat a path to their car.

Finally, a family from one of the upper income towns nearby called and after we carefully described Lokey to them, they advised us that they would be driving out for a look. They said he sounded like just what they were looking for. Over the phone, they seemed like the perfect family, so we crossed our fingers and held our breath in anticipation of their arrival.

When they arrived, their two young boys were out of their van and all over Lokey in a flash.

Tail traveling at warp speed, Lokey responded in kind, zeroing in on one son in particular. Dogs have a strange way of picking people and there is nothing more heartwarming than watching little boys and a dog coming together.

Later, we came to find that this search was all about one of the little boys. He was autistic, and his parents were anxious to find a four-legged friend to keep him company.

One might conclude that it was love at first sight because it was. Lokey zeroed in and spent most of his time fawning over that son.

Lokey must have sensed he was on the way out, or, unbeknown to us, had found and read our "parents wanted" ad in the pet classifieds.

If we didn't know better, we'd have concluded that the ingrate had packed his food bowls and bed and stashed them at the end of the driveway in order to make a quick getaway.

Within what seemed a matter of minutes, Lokey's new parents and two very happy little boys were being loaded into their minivan. As they headed up the hill toward the main road, we could see a very large, gold-colored dog happily seated in the back with the boys.

As Carla and I stood in the carport waving goodbye, we felt good about ourselves.

Our effort to find Lokey a good and permanent home appeared to be a smashing success. After having him as a loving house guest for several weeks, and then seeing him with that little boy, we were confident they would become very special friends, and create a friendship that would last for years. What more could we ask? Both of us were sure that the other had done the right thing — life doesn't get much better than that — does it?

The warmth we were feeling didn't last very long. As it turned out, we couldn't have been more wrong about sending Lokey away. Once that very happy family was out of sight we went inside, sat down at the kitchen table, took one look at each other, and the tears began to flow. Sometimes you don't grasp the enormity of what you've done, until after you've done it!

I don't know how they do it. It must be a gift. But whatever the magic, don't let anyone tell you that it takes years to become attached to a pet. Try, minutes, hours and days if you are a slow learner.

Pets begin tugging at your heart strings the moment they enter your life, and Lokey was no exception. Although he'd only been with us a short time, the big guy had left a hole in our hearts.

"Why did we give him up?" Carla sobbed.

"Because I thought you didn't want a dog, much less a big dog in a house filled with the cats," I responded.

Suddenly I found the buck being passed back to me.

"But I thought you didn't want a dog, didn't want the bother," she blurted out.

Well, the dastardly deed had been done. Both of us thought the other wanted to get rid of Lokey, and we had done just that. A good deed had been done and there was no turning back. Or was there?

Filling the Hole in Our Hearts

For the next week we moped around the house blaming each other for the state of misery that existed, it was as if a cloud had enveloped us. There was an emptiness in our hearts and in the carport where a four-legged stranger had sought refuge and stolen our hearts.

Another week passed, and we went down to Memphis for Christmas dinner with Carla's sister and her family. As misery has no boundaries, it came along for the ride.

Finally, I threw in the towel.

"Enough," I said. "Let's call the folks that took Lokey and offer to buy him back." I was hoping against hope that he was tearing their house apart, terrorizing the neighbors, or both.

I was wrong on both counts. Everyone loved Lokey. He was indeed man's best friend. He'd made the transition in the same way he'd joined us — flawlessly.

I explained that we'd made a terrible mistake, that neither of us realized how much the other had grown attached to him. I told them how much we missed Lokey from the moment we watched him going up the driveway in their van.

When this approach failed to achieve the desired result, I offered to buy Lokey's new parents a puppy of their choosing for their son, cost be damned.

Once again, I was shot down. The bond between their son and the dog was instant the day they met. I was told their decision was cast in stone.

Out of ammunition, so to speak, I gave up my quest and told them we understood. I wished everyone well, and, with my tail between my legs, I hung up the phone.

Lokey and the boy may have been happy, but in the days that followed, the misery index in our house continued to climb.

There was only one solution to the problem, so once again I stepped forward. I invited my wife to join me in the search for a puppy.

"What kind?" she asked.

Now that I'd experienced a large dog nothing else would do. I'm six foot three, two hundred pounds, and the last thing I wanted to be seen doing was walking down the road with a small, yappy dog on a leash.

Call it macho. Call it whatever you want, but remember, we were living in the country — living in an area where men were men, their dogs were dogs. And that's just the way it was!

Don't ask me why or how, but for some reason known only to God I suspect, I'd decided that the dog for me was a German shepherd. I didn't know anything about them. Didn't have a clue where to start my search or how to find a legitimate breeder. I just knew that that was what I had to have.

Now all we had to do was find the right pup.

My life with pets has been full of surprises. At least it seemed that way. First, there was a big dog, the answer to my childhood dreams. It lasted one day in our house.

With nary a thought about pets from this point forward, I finished college and began my business career. 23 years passed and suddenly I found myself surrounded by cats.

Cats! Cats were cold, unemotional and most important — small! I fed them and petted them, but could I learn to love them? Yes! Suddenly, I remembered Charlie Brown. He'd come into my life and blown me away.

Sure, I had become fond of our kittens when they arrived, but Charlie touched me as I had seldom if ever been touched, and my love for cats was off and running.

"Wolfie and Tony wrapped their paws around my heart. And then of course, there was Scrappy. As I reviewed the editor's comments for this story, it seemed as though, from out of the farthest corner of my mind I heard a gentle voice whisper, "don't forget me!" Scrappy had only been with us for about a week, but his courage and the love that grew as we tried to rehabilitate that little guy was beyond words. Scrappy, is one kitten that I will never forget.

If anyone had suggested to me that Carla and I would be beating the bushes, so to speak, in search of a puppy at this point in our lives, I'd have said they were nuts. A dog had always been the furthest thing from our minds.

We'd been cat people for nearly fifteen years. A dog — never in a million years!

Yet the hunt — and that's what it turned out to be — was about to begin.

Like most folks, I guess we could have started with a trip down to the local animal shelter or one of several pet stores in the immediate area in search of a puppy, but we didn't want just any pooch. We were looking for an American German shepherd.

Granted, we might get lucky and find a few pups at a pet store. However, from what we'd read, the reputation of their breeders was suspect.

A visit to a shelter might very well turn up one or more adult dogs of varying ages — dogs that had been turned in by their previous owners for one reason or another. Others, may have been mistreated or simply dumped and left to roam the streets, as had been the case with Lokey.

Pet store or shelter, in both instances we felt we'd be left with little or no knowledge of our pup's family background. That history, the quality of the breeder and the treatment of its parents, tells prospective buyers a good deal about the future temperament of a puppy.

It's important to learn as much as possible about any pet you're about to bring into your house, and even more so where pedigree breeds are concerned. Breeder background is critical; at least that's what we'd been led to believe. There are far too many puppy mills turning out one batch of puppies after another.

We'd read that whether you were looking for a puppy or a young adult, knowing as much as possible about its bloodline, care, and handling and parental disposition made a big difference in the mental makeup of a new canine friend.

When our newfound four-legged friend was going to grow up to weigh seventy-five to one hundred pounds, there was no doubt in our minds that gathering as much information as possible was important.

Don't let anyone kid you. Deciding you want a dog is a big decision, and making a mistake can not only break your heart, it can be very costly.

Unless you know exactly what you want, which we did, the choices can be endless. There are over one hundred breeds to choose from. They come in almost as many sizes, shapes, and colors. Add to this all the mixed breeds if a pedigree isn't important, and what do you have? Confusion!

You'd think that knowing what breed we wanted would make the hunt and selection easier. It didn't.

Visiting breeders had its drawbacks. It can be difficult differentiating between the puppy mills and professionals. Some people are breeding just to make a buck. Others are in it for the love of the breed, for show, and to find good homes for those pups that won't make it into the show or working ring.

When all else fails, there's always the "pet classifieds," but all of the same problems applied here.

The bottom line, we knew we had to ask a lot of questions and "kick more than a few tires" before picking a pup that we hoped was going to be with us for the rest of its life.

If it turned out that we were fortunate enough to have a litter to pick from — well, let me tell you — the selection task suddenly multiplies by the number of pups.

When you look down at several little fuzz balls, all squealing and reaching out to you, don't be surprised if you find that rather than pick one you want to take all of them home with you.

And no matter which puppy you select, life as you know it, as we were about to find out, would change forever.

But let's begin at the beginning.

Once we decided we couldn't live without a puppy, we began searching and developing a shopping list — several, in fact.

Shopping for a puppy is almost as complicated as preparing for the arrival of a new baby.

Think comparing a puppy to a baby is an unfair analogy?

You're probably right. Four-legged babies hit the ground running, and I do mean running.

They also come with a complete set of teeth. Although their baby teeth are small, they can do a lot of damage. Anything at eye level is fair game and they can do an amazing amount of damage in a matter of minutes. Arms, legs and ankles are fair game as well.

They enter the world with an explorer's curiosity. If it isn't tied down, they want to find it and take it away for closer observation.

You may laugh hysterically as your shoe or a small rug heads down the hall in their mouth, but after a while, well, you get the picture.

Make no mistake. A puppy is a living, breathing live action toy in hyper drive. Running is second nature to them. A sure sign that they have run out of gas, will find the little angels curled up on the floor or snuggled on your lap. At this point in our lives, our biggest concern was whether we could keep up as our child grew up.

My wife was in her mid-forties and I was in my mid fifties. We both thought we had had all the four-legged babies we wanted. As for the two-legged ones? They were nice, as long as they belonged to someone else. As you can see, we had questions. The answers would have to be addressed at some future time.

To sum up the act of puppy shopping in as few words as possible, we found it to be like Christmas in July. We found ourselves making lists, one after another.

We did our best to identify everything we thought we'd need, and when we weren't sure, we added those items to one list or another.

The only immediate benefit that comes to mind when bringing a puppy into your home is the fact that you don't have to buy clothes or paint a room blue or pink. I guess you could, but why would you?

However, having been a Boy Scout, I wanted to "be prepared."

Puppies are usually small, wriggly things, so at the top of our shopping list was a pet carrier for initial trips to the vet.

Next, we felt we needed two crates, a smaller one for housebreaking and a larger one for traveling and future growth.

A crate would provide a safe place for our cuddly canine to sleep. When we were traveling it would insure that hotel people would remain "happy campers" when they came in to calculate the damage done and found there was none.

From everything we'd read, crates and wire kennel carriers were valuable teaching aids when a pup required a "time out" or we left the house for a few hours.

They say dogs won't mess where they sleep. We determined that the two crates, one small and the other large, for use later, would go a long way toward instilling the right manners in our future pooch while protecting expensive carpeting and area rugs.

During these unplanned emergencies we were told that you needed a quick, sharp voice command and an even quicker reaction as you rushed for a leash, hooked puppy up and dashed through the house and out to the lawn. Care to bet on your chances?

When it was bedtime, we wanted a soft, fluffy bed for our pup to snuggle up in and catch some Zs. We had no intention of allowing the little tyke to sleep on a cold, hard floor.

Next on our list were puppy toys. Do you have any idea how many toys are available for pets? The squeaky and chew toys in assorted sizes and shapes will keep you reaching for your wallet throughout the life of your new family member.

Unless we were willing to watch our furniture being destroyed — and we weren't — chew toys were a must. They don't come with a guarantee to replace furniture and other personal items, but as they say, "An ounce of prevention."

What to feed a pup, though not an immediate priority, called for another list. Since we didn't know how long it would take to find the right child we decided to prepare in advance.

As with toys, the meal selection went on and on. There was puppy food for specific breeds, sizes, stomachs, and ages — so many choices. It was akin to visiting a gourmet restaurant — offered in cans and bags.

How do you satisfy a hungry pup's cravings? As we would soon find out, it was trial and error. *Bon appetite*, as they say. What you see on television doesn't begin to scratch the surface where choices are concerned. The menu selection is endless. And don't be surprised if your furry friend has a gourmet's palate and refuses your initial choices.

And what pet doesn't need vitamins, dog treats, and assorted digestible chews?

When it's time to take the love of your life for a walk, you'll need a collar and leash. As we reviewed our options we discovered that not just any collar and leash would do. We'd want one that defined our child. Color for gender, red or pink — in our case a female. There were even collars with sparkling jewels and/or metal studs, for show and further male/female identification.

We knew that whatever items we chose would be replaced several times over as junior grew up, but cost never entered the picture.

While we were cruising up and down the local pet store aisles we noted an array of reading material for new and potential pet owners.

We knew the breed we wanted, and as we perused pet and bookstore shelves we found that when it came to bringing up and living with baby, the "How To" and "Why Not" theories that spoke to training and co-existing with a new pet were as varied as the selection of food and toys.

Because I had my heart set on a German shepherd, we picked up several books that described the breed — how smart, loyal, and loving they were. One book in particular, written by the Monks at the New Skete Monastery in upstate New York, would ultimately become our bible. Although the monks trained all breeds for owners willing to make the trip and leave their dogs for several weeks, they were best known for breeding, training and selling German shepherds.

Their book covered every facet of the puppy to adult experience with particular attention paid to house training, an area known to drive new puppy owners to distraction.

They covered all of the key training areas: sit, stay, down, come, fetch and return and the importance of not greeting guests by jumping up and bowling them over. Their recommendations were great in theory, but, more about that later.

We didn't realize just how famous the Monks of New Skete were until one day when we saw their show listed in our TV guide. Their program was on for several weeks and showed their skills working with all dogs, large and small — and of course, German shepherds. We taped a number of programs so that we could refer back to specific training and obedience issues. If you think our effort to prepare in advance for a new arrival was complete, think again.

Babies require periodic checkups. So do pups. We had no idea how long our search for a pup would take, but we knew we needed to have a vet standing by.

Fortunately we had a vet for the cats. Otherwise, we could imagine how a new pet owner feels as they talk to other pet owners and run through the listings in the local telephone directory looking for a vet. At times, this turned out to be costly and frustrating as we searched for one that we felt comfortable with.

Over the years we'd found that board certification when selecting a vet was a plus. However, in the end, it really came down to meeting with and talking to several local vets. Ask around, and you'll find that every dog and cat owner you come in contact with has a vet story to tell.

Selection of pre-school and continuing education was high on our list once we found a pup. You heard right, and picking the right school for training your newfound friend is like picking a vet. It takes time and, you guessed it, trial and error.

Obedience training was important to us. We wanted to find a professional trainer, one with solid credentials, a well thought out program and good training facilities. There are any number of people available to new dog owners that call themselves trainers, but believe me, many of them aren't! Don't be surprised if you go through one or two before finding the right one.

Our four-legged pets don't come hardwired to sit, stay, heel, come, and lie down on command. Socialization, the opportunity to meet other pets on the street without having your arm torn from its socket, requires training, patience and plenty of practice. Failure to instill the social graces in your little charger will require very strong arms and, although shouting and screaming seldom work, regular use of the words *no* and *stop* will go a long way to achieving the right result.

The more we read and watched others, the more we became convinced that that dainty little pup, the love of your life, has the strength of Hercules when he or she wants to demonstrate who runs the sidewalk.

We knew it would take time to instill good manners inside the home, as well as outdoors. It was either that or plan to get a good grip on the leash as pooch attempted to haul one of us down the street in order to challenge every canine in the neighborhood.

There was no doubt about it, if we expected our child to strut her stuff and show off how well-mannered she was, we knew that finding a professional trainer was an absolute necessity.

Setting aside the time to work with the trainer and then with our pup, one on one, was going to require sacrifice. Fortunately, we were retired, so that made the task easier.

Pet owners we met told us not to give up if our first trainer failed to succeed in transforming our little charger into Miss Manners.

As it turned out, we didn't realize how many trainers we'd have to go through before we found one able to curb our child's enthusiasm. You can count on the fact that it is not as easy as the local pet store trainer makes it look. His classes may provide a starting point but don't be surprised if reaching the finish line, with your pup at your side, requires additional training.

We learned the hard way that just because your pup shows signs of brilliance in a class setting is no guarantee that once out the door all won't be forgotten.

Finding the perfect pup proved to be no simple task. Breeders and trainers fell by the wayside during our first expedition into the world of doggy-dom.

Searching for Ms. Right

Because we wanted an American German shepherd, we ruled out pet stores and started watching the local newspaper classifieds, expecting to find any number of "pets for sale" ads.

As expected, there was an ample supply of puppies available. However, in our neck of the woods that meant Labs, Golden Retrievers, other hunting dogs, and, of course, the usual array of yappy, ankle-high specimens. You know the ones I mean, those requiring frizzy hairdos.

German shepherds were few and far between.

I'm relating our adventure so that you won't be discouraged if you don't find what you're looking for in a matter of days. We didn't.

Our search was well into its second month, and all we had to show for our effort was an ever-growing pile of dog supplies and a number of books dealing with how to raise, enjoy, and learn to live with a German shepherd.

Several weeks of searching had only turned up a couple of litters of white shepherds. They were different, but for one reason or another, they just didn't strike a chord and melt our hearts.

Maybe it was because they didn't look like what we felt German shepherds were supposed to look like. Matter a fact they looked like they should have been pulling sleds in the Yukon.

In both instances, the white shepherds we visited were huge. When the breeder took us back to look at his pups, mom and dad demonstrated their displeasure at seeing us near their children There was plenty of growling and lunging at the wire fences that separated us. That display clinched it for us. White just wasn't right.

Years later we learned that gentle parents and good breeding and upbringing while in the hands of the breeder went a long way toward producing lovable puppies and subsequent adults.

Finally, we spotted an ad for American German shepherd puppies in a small town newspaper about twenty-five miles away.

According to the ad, the breeder had two females remaining from a recent litter. The pups were nine weeks old and ready for a new home.

We'd already decided we wanted a female as they tended to be a little smaller and more even tempered.

We called for directions and learned a little more about the puppies, including the fact that the breeding pair was owned by the breeder, which isn't always the case, and the pups would be AKC registered. Novices that we were, we saw this as being tantamount to a Good Housekeeping seal of approval.

Our first visit was informative and uneventful. We met the parents, and — although we weren't greeted with open arms when we looked at the pups — we didn't come away glad there was a fence separating us.

As for the two girls, one was rambunctious, bordering on aggressive, while the other seemed very reserved and standoffish as she tried to hide in the furthest corner of the puppy pen.

We spent about an hour talking with the breeder and watching the pups and learned that she intended to keep whichever girl remained, as she and her daughter lived alone, and she wanted an in-house pet for protection.

She told us that she'd been breeding shepherds for several years, and from what we could see, she was not running a puppy mill. The kennels were neat and clean.

Her breeding pair lived in a fenced kennel area behind the house, and although they might bark and growl if they sensed an intruder, because they weren't allowed in the house, they afforded the breeder little more than an early warning system.

The price for a puppy was $250.00 including AKC papers and registration forms. At the time this seemed like a lot of money for a dog, but considering the lack of American German shepherds to choose from, I concluded this wasn't going to deter us.

Taking on a new mouth to feed, one that we hoped would be with us for a long time, required discussion. So once the breeder had satisfied all of our immediate questions, we thanked her and went home to put our heads together.

Were we sure we wanted to do this?

Absolutely! We'd been moping around the house ever since we watched Lokey going up the hill and out of our lives.

Would the addition of a puppy cause chaos within the empire?

Without a doubt! Our pup wouldn't remain small forever. Eventually she would grow up, and in this instance our little girl was destined to become a large dog. This, we were sure, would not go over well with our felines.

Most importantly, we wanted her to be an in-house member of the family. If we were going to have a dog, I wanted it within arm's reach.

As far as I was concerned, a dog — and for that matter, all dogs and cats — were put on this earth for petting, one-sided discussions with their owners, love, and affection.

For years our cats had ruled the roost in our house with iron paws. Suddenly, we were about to make a change that was sure to be traumatic for our finicky felines.

After all, if you were a cat what would you think? One minute you're king of the hill, and the next you're chopped liver!

After several years of living with cats, we were sure their little minds would conclude that they had fallen from grace, which was hardly the case. But have you ever tried to reason with a cat?

All of our cats but one were Oriental shorthairs. They didn't understand English. How did we know? How many cats have you known that pay attention to commands.

Unlike dogs, cats come and go, ignoring their owners whenever a response is inconvenient. They march to their own drummer.

As we didn't understand any of the Asian languages, we were sure that most of the comments coming from our band of spoiled Orientals, upon seeing a dog in the house, wouldn't be fit to print.

There was only one answer where the subject of co-existence was concerned — the cats would just have to get over it!

Would our lifestyle change?

We weren't sure, but we decided to soldier on.

After years living with cats, we'd come to the happy conclusion that they're independent, self-cleaning pets. Not so with a dog.

You don't adopt cats under the false pretense that they'll be sitting next to you on the couch every night or shower you with licks and squeals of joy when you came through the door after being gone for several hours.

Where cats are concerned, any show of affection is always a pleasant surprise.

The nice thing about cats is that you can leave them for days at a time as long as someone comes in to feed them, clean their litter box, and provide a fresh bowl of water.

From what we'd read, dogs, on the other hand — and puppies in particular — had feelings — real feelings — that required nurturing.

As it turned out, whoever said or wrote that knew what he was talking about!

Leave a puppy alone for a few minutes and the moans, groans, howls, and cries will lead your neighbors to believe you are an axe murderer.

Our last question involved the cost of the pup.

We'd already spent a fortune on toys, food, beds, books, carriers, and the like, so who was keeping track?

Besides, when you're already feeding eight little mouths every day, what's one more? Even though the mouth in question and corresponding appetite will, over time, surpass the feeding needs of the other eight.

Having arrived at satisfactory answers to all of our questions, concerns, and soul-searching it was obvious that nothing was going to alter our desire for a pup.

Within a few days we were back on the phone with the breeder checking to see if the two girls were still available. They were. So we grabbed our largest cat carrier, jumped in my wife's minivan, and headed out to claim our new child and begin our journey through canine parenthood.

Of the two girls, we'd pretty much concluded that the shy girl was our choice. This, of course, was subject to some additional discussion with the breeder.

At first glance and based upon everything we had read, we hoped that the shy, more hesitant child would fit our slow, rather laid back lifestyle. The last thing we needed was a hyper hound with energy to burn. Retirement, remember?

Of course, there are no guarantees when selecting a pet that it will match your lifestyle. First impressions are important, but only time and a knowledgeable breeder would tell — we hoped.

Compared to her energetic and aggressive sibling, already dubbed by us "the ugly sister," our potential child was not only angelic; she was beautiful, as once again, she tried to disappear into the furthest corner of the play area. Ah, parenthood!

Once again, we pulled up chairs in the backyard and, without telling the breeder our choice, repeated our desire to find a very submissive female rather than one that evidenced a high degree of emotion and energy.

"Tell us," we asked, "knowing our needs, which of the pups would you select and why?"

As it turned out, our choice was hers as well.

I guess there's something to be said for knowing you've got a sale in hand that brings out the best in a seller. In this case, the breeder was all smiles. She couldn't stop singing the praises of the laid back pup.

"That little girl, the one sitting in the back of the puppy pen, that's the one you want. I really think she's going to turn out to be a very mellow adult."

Based upon the fact that she had bred and shown German shepherds for several years, we took the breeder at her word.

However, looking back on that moment, I think we probably asked and answered our own question for the breeder.

"We'll take her," we both responded.

"I'm glad she's your choice. I was hoping to keep the other girl," she responded. Said future guard dog was in the process of trying to climb the wire fence and attack. "She's definitely a high energy pup and should make a good watchdog as well as a great pet."

That was fine with us; we wanted a pup we could love, spoil, and enjoy without worrying about visitors being attacked as they came through our front door.

Of course, if before opening the door, unwanted visitors were greeted with a growl that shook the ground and sent shock waves up and down their spines, that was just fine with us.

Once we acknowledged our guests, we expected them to be greeted by our child with tail wags and licks. Jumping would be forbidden.

With all of our questions asked and answered, many for the second time, we completed the purchase of our new little girl, who from this day forward would be called, "Sabrina."

She was black and tan in all the right places, with a beautiful V-shaped tan marking that began at her forehead and ran down between her eyes. It ended at what was very definitely a German shepherd head and nose.

Sabrina might have been a puppy, but she was quite a load for nine weeks, weighing twenty-four pounds. Years later we learned that she was big, really big for her age.

With huge paws and large floppy ears, she looked more like a baby bear than a German shepherd. Later, her paws would cause everyone that saw her to exclaim, "Get a load of those feet! She's going to be big girl, really big."

Such comments may have brought a smile to our faces, but to a young lady like Sabrina, I'm sure that was the last thing she wanted to hear. Good thing her vocabulary was a work in progress.

Her mother and father weren't small. Dad weighed over one hundred pounds and Mom exceeded ninety, so we weren't at all surprised by early predictions of her future weight.

We stuffed, and I do mean stuffed, our over-sized fuzz ball into the carrier we'd brought along, placed her on the back seat of the van and, having said our goodbyes, headed for home.

We hadn't gone far when it became apparent that Sabrina needed breathing room, so I opened the carrier door and allowed her access to the backseat.

Before I could yell, "No, stop, Sabrina," not that she knew her name or the word *stop*, we heard sounds that could only mean one thing: car sickness. Apparently that wasn't covered in any of our books or the discussions we'd had with the breeder.

By the time we made our way out of traffic and over to the side of the road, the backseat and floor of Carla's new minivan had been christened — and this was no small christening.

It's amazing how much "stuff" can come up from the stomach of a puppy.

Amidst a variety of expletives not fit to print, words that by no stretch of the imagination could be considered praise, my wife dug a roll of paper towels out from a rear storage bin and commenced a temporary cleanup.

If all eight of our cats pitched hairballs at the same time, they wouldn't have equaled Sabrina's initial entry into our family.

Just in case you don't know it: beware, it's impossible to get mad at a puppy. God won't allow it. In fact, I'm sure he's made it a point to provide each and every dog and cat that comes into this world with a "Did I do that?" look to be used for just such occasions.

That look combined with the cocking of the head first right and then left, as we "vented" our anger at a child that didn't understand a word we were shrieking, won the day. The madder we got, the more we smiled. Before long we'd forgotten why we were mad and were taking turns cuddling the perpetrator!

Carla finished cleaning up as I stood by the side of the car with Sabrina, waiting to continue our journey home.

Once everyone was seated again and with the windows partially open to provide some much needed fresh air, we completed an uneventful drive home with our new child.

Over the years I've often wondered what our child was thinking at any given moment.

As we drove home that afternoon, I could almost hear her saying to herself, "*Gee, that went over well!*"

Welcome to the family, Sabrina!

Living with Baby

Ah, parenthood!

The next stage of the rest of our lives with Sabrina was about to begin!

Looking back, that's about how we felt. In reality, Sabrina's growing up period only lasted about eighteen months. We lived through it, but there were times when we were sure her being a puppy would never end.

She wasn't a mischievous or destructive child, she was just a puppy. Lots of curiosity, carrying on and the constant desire to stay as close to us as possible, required that we step lightly in order to avoid injuring a paw or tail.

Our house was built on several levels with steps leading from one level to the next. Fortunately, there were no more than three steps separating any level except the loft above the family room. This was my "escape to peace and quiet" room. It was also where I had my office.

The open wood steps leading to this second story loft kept Sabrina and the cats down below. No matter how much she or the cats wanted to join me when I was working, those open steps seemed to deter them.

Most of the floors in the house were hardwood or tile, with only the master bedroom carpeted. The hardwood floors served as a launching pad for the newest member of the family.

When traveling from one end of the house to the other, our little tyke would pause, take a deep breath, gather herself for launch, and then take off.

I never doubted the fact that she saw herself as a four-legged aviator. "*Brakes locked. Throttle forward and release — jeez, what a blast!*"

With a good head of steam, she could launch herself off one set of steps after another as she raced to her destination.

Her aircraft carrier landings and takeoffs were a sight to behold. She would soar off a top step and arrive at her destination with her wheels (legs) splayed, just in time for a belly landing and a skidding halt. Most stops were compliments of a wall or a piece of furniture.

Upon stopping, she'd stand, shake off the effects of the harder landings, then check to make sure she was all there.

After taking a moment to catch her breath and regroup, she'd continue on her way with us seldom, if ever, knowing her final destination or what prompted these flights of fancy.

When she wasn't soaring two feet above her universe, she was exploring. No nook or cranny was left untouched by her ever lengthening nose.

You've heard of baby proofing? Well, let me tell you, puppy proofing takes the art of "Where can we put this or that?" to a whole new level.

If it wasn't nailed down or out of reach of Sabrina's constantly changing dimensions, it ended up in her mouth as she beat a path away from its assigned place with her latest prize.

The words *no*, *come*, and *Sabrina, stop* became her battle cry to ignore. That's what puppies do. They look, listen, and then if they think they can get away with whatever they're doing, they carry on.

Their sole task during this early stage of their life is to see everything, see how much they can get away with, and see how little they have to pay attention.

Does this mean to imply that our child was dumb? Absolutely not! She was smart like a fox, or as her mother put it, "Well on the way to being spoiled rotten by her evil father."

Sabrina knew what to do when trapped with evidence in her mouth or being dragged behind her. She would immediately put on her best "Who me?" face, or better yet, roll over on her back in an act of submission, prepared to allow us to rub her belly rather than smack her butt. These defensive weapons worked every time.

Sabrina's initial nights in her new digs were enough to wake the neighbors, if we had any within ear shot, which we didn't. Each of the three houses near us had over an acre of property — the only folks she kept up were the parents. So much noise from such a small body!

Our initial sleeping arrangement involved tethering her to a leg of the bed on a short leash. We'd read that if she could hear us breathing and sleep on the same blanket or towels night after night, thus capturing her scent, this would reassure and comfort her. It didn't.

During those initial nights, in an effort to keep from having to clean up accidents in the house, my wife and I could be found with flashlight and flags, wandering around our front yard with Sabrina leading the way. I've yet to understand why we considered every howl or cry after the lights went out to be a request to go outside, but we did.

On the other hand, our spoiled child probably was saying to herself, "*Let's see, if I make a little noise they'll take me out and play with me.*"

As for the flags, they were the little red and orange ones similar to those construction people use to mark specific areas where they're working. You'd be surprised how many times those flags saved us from stepping on a pile in the middle of the night.

Each trip outdoors was a repeat of the last. First our little sentry would mark a new spot. Then she would look and listen, prepared to defend us. Meanwhile, we would stand at the end of the leash cold and tired, exhorting her over and over again to "do it." Eventually, she would attempt to please us by appearing to do something, thereby allowing us to go back to sleep.

At times it seemed as though we were taking her out every hour on the hour. This call for help worked for a while, but only for a while. After several sleepless nights, Carla and I had been reduced to walking zombies. There had to be a better idea, and there was!

Suddenly we remembered the New Skete Monks suggestion to use a crate for housebreaking and sleeping. I don't know why we didn't start with it right away, having purchased a crate even before our little girl arrived, but we didn't. Silly us!

It took a few days for Sabrina to get comfortable in the crate. However, before long, we found ourselves extending our hours of sleep per the schedule recommended in the book. Eight hours of sleep. You just can't beat it!

Extending the crate hours during the day and when it was time for a nap tended to remind and reinforce our message to Sabrina that her bathroom was outdoors.

Lo and behold, the monks were right. The crate became her second home. Before we knew it, Sabrina was toilet trained, sleeping, and napping on command.

Over the years we would joke, almost admiringly, that she had a bladder of steel, as her sleep and "holding" period extended beyond ten hours.

Thank the Lord!

Once we felt we could trust her, we attacked the next hurdle, leaving her to roam the house alone for an hour or two at a time while we left to run errands.

This worked well for a while. Then one day we came home to find that it had snowed feathers in our bedroom and entryway.

We'd forgotten to close the door to the bedroom, and our detective first class, sensing an opportunity for mischief, managed to find and explore the innards of my feather pillow.

Thinking like a puppy, I can imagine her saying, "*I smell a chicken. Come out, come out wherever you are. I know you're in there, this nose is never wrong.*"

To her dismay, she didn't find the chicken, goose, or duck she thought was inside the pillow. However, this wasn't from a lack of trying. By the time Sabrina was through shaking the living stuffing out of that pillow, our bedroom and entryway was coated with feathers.

You'd be surprised how many feathers can be stuffed in a pillow. We were.

We didn't know whether to laugh or cry. I mean, after all, we were as guilty as she was, having left the bedroom door open.

So rather than cry over spilled feathers, we commenced to sweep and vacuum them up. The fact that it took days to find all of them served as a reminder. We wouldn't make the same mistake a second time.

One of the nice things about a crate is the fact that once your little charge gets used to it, you can employ it for a variety of tasks.

Heading the list was being able to leave the house for hours without having to worry about the level of destruction you could expect to find upon your return.

Unlike children, much to the chagrin of their owners, dogs grow to their full size at a rapid rate. Sabrina was no exception. Before we knew it, our bouncing baby girl wasn't a baby anymore and was in need of a much larger crate. Sabrina was a full-grown, seventy-five-pound German shepherd.

Shepherds have very distinctive, large pointed ears, ears that are usually up well before their growing cycle is complete. Not our girl.

For several months everything grew, including her ears. However, the ears stayed down on the side of her head. They refused to stand up.

When she ran, she looked like the flying nun readying for liftoff, as her ears flapped in the breeze.

Suddenly, one ear went up. Then that ear came down, and the other ear went up. Finally, after what seemed an eternity, we woke one morning to find that both of her large, beautifully pointed ears were standing straight up where they belonged. At last, our little girl had become a full-fledged German shepherd.

Greetings in our house usually included a hug. Sabrina, not wanting to be overlooked where affection was concerned, would come charging across the house squealing for joy when a hug was in progress. She'd stand on her hind legs, rising to her full height, and join in what became known as a "group hug."

I should point out that I'm six foot three, and Sabrina, when standing on her hind legs, could look me in the eyes.

Remember our cats?

Well, that part of our adventure didn't go quite as planned.

When we introduced Sabrina, the puppy, to the cats, their abandon-ship drill went into fast forward. Before we knew it, all the felines were safe, out of harm's way, breathing hard but resting atop their cages as they looked down at a winded and tail-wagging Sabrina.

We never quite understood why our attempt to bring our children together didn't work. Maybe it was Sabrina's large feet that scared them, or the fact that even as a puppy she was three times the size of our largest cat.

Then again, quite possibly her barking reminded our spoiled brats that cats and dogs don't mix.

Sabrina did her best to become a good neighbor. She never stopped charging after the cats in an effort to introduce herself.

To her, I'm sure that everything with four legs had to be a dog.

The cats, on the other hand, did their best to become invisible.

If they lacked enthusiasm for a new sister and were shocked at her size when they saw her for the first time, they had to be dismayed with every day that passed. There, before their very eyes, was this thing that barked, that seemed to be growing larger by the hour.

I'm sure their bedtime prayers included a request to make it, whatever it was, go away.

One of our females had been moved to our room as she was on the verge of delivering kittens.

Ah hah, we thought, *maybe the kittens will feel comfortable with Sabrina and that will rub off on the others.*

This turned out to be another good idea that didn't pan out.

Sabrina loved the kittens from the moment they arrived and showed her affection with licks, tail wags, and cries of joy.

Sadly she was also prone to placing her size fourteens on them in order to hold them in place for a lick.

When she wasn't attempting to hold them down, she was trying to take them for a ride in her mouth.

This didn't sit well with Carla. I kept saying, "Don't worry. She won't eat them," but even if this show of affection was driven by love, who could be sure? One accidental swallow and a kitten would be history.

In this instance, an ounce of prevention turned out to be the order of the day.

So with her transition from fuzz ball puppy to full-size German shepherd taking shape on a daily basis, it became obvious to us that our newest child would have to be separated from her newfound furry feline family.

Separation became the name of the game. The cats would have time out of the cattery each day.

Sabrina would have plenty of time with us as well. However, when the cats were out, she would be relegated to her crate.

While on the subject of growing — in case you've never taken an untrained, full-grown shepherd for a walk — let me tell you, our first walks were an adventure, especially since we lived in the country.

Nothing escaped the eyes and ears of my girl. Every leaf, every bird, every anything that moved was a call to stop, identify, then charge.

I would hold on and attempt to dig my heels into the ground, all the while yelling "*no*." Sabrina, in turn, would do her best to ignore my cries as she attempted to give exploration her undivided attention.

Think powerful cars and trucks having torque? When she had her body in gear in order to take a closer look at whatever motivated her, she was an express train on the move.

If her fuse was lit as we were coming down the hill to our house, my life on more than one occasion flashed before my eyes. It took all the strength I could muster to avoid going end over end, over the edge, headlong into the trees at the bottom of the hill.

It was during expeditions to pick up the mail or just to get in some exercise that the need for schooling became painfully obvious. The more we walked the more convinced I became that she was allowing me to go for a walk with her, rather than the other way around.

Picking up the mail involved a quarter-mile hike to the mailbox. On the way, this included a daily stop to visit with Dandelion.

Who is Dandelion, you ask?

She was the pet pig that one of our neighbors had bought for their kids to raise.

I'm sure Sabrina concluded, "*That's the ugliest dog I've ever seen. Smells funny too!*"

Over time, Dandelion and Sabrina became fast friends. No matter where that porker was when we arrived at her fenced-in area, she would come trundling over and go snout to nose with Sabrina.

One day Dandelion failed to appear. Sabrina looked everywhere, paced back and forth, barked and cried out, all to no avail. Unbeknown to her, Dandelion had gone to meet her maker — the maker of pork chops, ribs, and sausage.

However, Dandelion left a lasting impression. All of the neighbors enjoyed a part of her. The fact that she had been raised on Hostess Twinkies, cupcakes, and other assorted sweets from the local thrift store made her sausage among the best I have ever tasted.

Feeling the loss of a friend or relative is not foreign to our pets.

For weeks she would stop at the fence, bark and wait for Dandelion to come running, but of course, she never came. Then one morning she didn't stop. The grieving was over. Fortunately, she would meet new friends as we took our daily walks.

Our little girl loved ice cream. So until we discovered she had irritable bowel syndrome and was lactose intolerant, she would join us on our trips to town to the local Dairy Queen.

All she had to see was us heading to the front door with her aluminum bowl in hand, and she was front and center, waiting for the car door to open so she could take up her position as guardian of the backseat.

Once at the DQ, that beautiful head of hers would make itself known as soon as her window was rolled down. Everyone at the drive-thru knew her. They thought it was funny to see a German shepherd with a big smile, waiting patiently as they filled her bowl with frozen custard.

Sabrina didn't see the humor in their laughter, but she sure enjoyed the end result.

When we were out for serious exercise, Sabrina and I would turn on to the secondary road where the mail boxes were lined up and head for the main road.

This, in turn, often resulted in Sabrina visiting with her newest buddies.

Another neighbor had purchased a small herd of goats, and Sabrina, believing everyone was put on earth for her to befriend, did just that.

When the goats or one of the herding dogs that watched them escaped their fenced area, it wasn't unusual for us to find them standing in our carport wondering when Sabrina could come out to play.

Going for a walk with Sabrina provided an opportunity to commune with nature. It made no difference whether critters were fenced in or loose, she wanted to meet them all. As far as she was concerned, I was simply along for the ride.

One day our next-door neighbor brought home a male yellow Labrador puppy he'd named Tucker.

As I recall, it wasn't love at first sight. As far as Sabrina was concerned, this newcomer was a dork. Of course, our little beauty queen failed to recall what she looked like when we brought her home. Oh, thee of failing memory!

When the two pups were introduced, she turned up her nose. My girl wanted nothing to do with Tucker. However, in a matter of months, as Tucker grew to full size, Sabrina's interest was piqued.

Tucker, the dork, became her knight in shining armor.

The two dogs became fast friends.

Watching the two youngsters play was quite a sight.

Because Sabrina was never off leash, we strung a hundred feet of clothesline between two trees. Then we placed an eye on the line that allowed her to move back and forth.

When Sabrina went out to play with Tucker, her thirty-foot leash, attached to the eye, provided her with plenty of room to run and roll around.

Whenever we went for a walk, Tucker would suddenly and mysteriously materialize. The two dogs would walk side by side, Sabrina on her leash, Tucker strutting freely at her side.

They were the equivalent of two inseparable humans out for a stroll. It's too bad they had paws and not hands; otherwise I'm sure they would have been walking hand in hand. Ah, young love.

Tucker knew that Sabrina couldn't have pups, but that didn't seem to faze him. He was her man, and she was his bud.

If ever there was a happy-go-lucky pup, it was Tucker, otherwise known in the neighborhood as — " Dillinger."

Where Sabrina liked to check out new things, Tucker enjoyed taking them. Anything left outside was fair game.

From work boots to flowerpots, with or without flowers, and even twenty-pound bags of soil, nothing stopped this happy-go-lucky thief.

We, in turn, would walk next door in search of whatever was missing. If we couldn't find it, we'd leave a note on the front door, and before we knew it, it was returned.

However, just as with Dandelion, one day Tucker was nowhere to be seen.

Sabrina looked all over as we walked, expecting Tucker to come bounding across the fields to see his buddy and mooch a couple of the dog biscuits he knew I carried in my coat pocket especially for him.

But on this particular day, it was not to be.

I've never been able to understand the logic of putting a dog on a leash, then attaching the leash to something in the bed of a pickup truck. It might look very "down home and country," but the idea of a rear-end collision or sudden stop harming the dog always seemed to me to be a distinct possibility.

One day, possibility became a reality.

The truck Tucker was riding in stopped quickly, and he didn't. Tucker was thrown out of the bed and strangled by the leash.

What a waste. What a tragic waste of a wonderful, fun-loving, and well-behaved friend.

If our pets respond to tragedies, as I suspect they do, then this was Sabrina's second one. I found her looking for Tucker every time we were outside. Walks saw her head constantly moving from side to side looking for him — expecting him to come bounding across the field to be by her side — but to no avail. Her Tucker was gone and I'm sure she couldn't understand why.

If you get the idea that Sabrina, like most humans, had many friends, you're right. Sadly, not all of them were around to see her off when the time came for us to depart for her new home in Florida. But that adventure will come later.

Thinking back on our stay in the country, I don't think Sabrina had a mean bone in her body. She loved everyone and every living thing from the day she was born. In turn, all she demanded was that everyone love her as much as she loved them.

It didn't always work out that way with the deer, squirrels, wild turkeys, ducks, and geese that frequented our front yard, but our girl never stopped trying to get acquainted with every visitor.

Over time we'd been able to teach Sabrina a few commands, but only one of them garnered the proper response every time. All I had to do was look at her as I walked by, and say, "want to go for a ride with me?" Instantly, she would be up and running to the door leading to our car. Once out the door and dragging her leash behind, she would position herself at the back door of the car and look back wondering what was taking me so long.

I began taking Sabrina with me most every time I had an errand to run. Once on the back seat, affectionately known as "her post," we'd be off to the car wash, to fill the up with gas, drop a book at the library's outside return box or, of course, to the bank.

The bank was her favorite stop. We always went to the drive-thru window. Once there, I would drop the rear window down and Sabrina would lean out and wait for what she knew was coming, two large dog biscuits. Most everyone that worked the window knew her name.

If the two of us were off on an errand and someone called the house to talk with me, Carla's response was always the same, "the boy and his dog are off in the car, I'll have him call you when he returns."

At times, it probably seemed to Carla and our friends, that Sabrina and I were inseparable.

My little girl may have grown in size as our trips in the car continued, but, she was a puppy at heart, a state of mind that would remain one of her endearing qualities — throughout her life with us.

Today, those romps to say hello to everything and everyone, with me holding on to the end of her leash for dear life, are fond memories.

At the time these daring dashes served to convince me that our child needed to understand the terms *boundaries* and *limitations*. She needed a pack leader.

She needed the S word — schooling!

School Days

There she sat. Her back legs tucked in. Back ramrod straight. She was sitting up tall. Eyes forward. She looked like a picture out of a German shepherd training manual.

Ah, graduation day, the culmination of all our hard work had paid off. We'd survived it, together.

I was the new pack leader and Sabrina was my pack — or so I thought.

There would be no long speeches. Caps wouldn't be thrown into the air.

Maybe a bark or two would replace the cheers normally associated with such festivities once the ceremony ended.

Yep, there was my little girl, surrounded by her classmates, anxiously awaiting those important words, "Congratulations. Today you've graduated."

As I looked down at her, she looked up and smiled as if to say, "*Wow, Mom and Dad sure must be proud. Are they in for a surprise!*"

We'd worked hard together. We'd practiced on almost a daily basis. This lasted the full six weeks of schooling and made graduation day all the more special. I couldn't have been more thrilled at the progress we made.

Instead of mortarboards with tassels, the graduates were wearing pointy party hats held on their heads by rubber bands. However, that didn't lessen the pride of the parents that stood beaming from ear to ear as they watched the ceremony; cameras in hand, flashes of light going off at a rapid rate — this was a Kodak moment — one that we captured on videotape and watched time and again as we asked ourselves — "whatever happened to all of that schooling?"

Unlike their first day at school, almost all of the graduates were calm. Hardly a growl or bark broke the solemnity of the event.

Chances are you think I'm getting ahead of myself, and I guess I am. So I'll step back and tell you how Sabrina, her mother, and I arrived at this most important moment.

I'm sure there comes a time in every puppy owner's life when he realizes that no matter how hard he tries, he just doesn't seem to be speaking his pup's language.

In our case, shouts of: no, stop, Sabrina, and come, were going unheeded most of the time. Even the more gentle commands, down and sit, seemed to be going in one ear and out the other.

Was our child deaf? We didn't think so.

She could hear me whisper, "Want a treat?" from the far end of the house and come running.

So after what seemed an eternity trying to train her, we began checking local pet stores to see if anyone offered socialization and obedience classes.

We knew Sabrina was smart. It said so in the books we'd read. "German shepherds are smart." Yet, for whatever reason, her attention span seemed equal to that of an ant.

At five months we were convinced she was old enough to demonstrate just how smart German shepherds were known to be.

She'd already proven to be the most relaxed, even tempered, sweetest four-legged child we had ever met.

Her breeder was right. No matter what anyone did to her, even the vet, she always came away smiling. There wasn't a mean bone in her body.

But when it came to paying attention, one of us definitely had a communication problem, and I knew it wasn't me.

Sure enough, one of the pet store chains offered a six-week course in socialization and basic obedience.

Carla and I drove the twenty miles to the store and watched one of the sessions.

An area in the center of the store, big enough to allow eight pups to move around, with chairs for the parents to sit when necessary, had been laid out in a circle and dubbed the classroom.

As we watched a class in session we concluded that this was a hand's-on course, with each parent working his or her dog.

We watched as the owners walked their little charges around in circles and took them through the various commands and requests of the trainer.

Owners took turns walking their dogs up to each individual classmate for a get-acquainted sniff. This obviously was part of the socialization process, and even this seemed to be going reasonably well.

Of course, whether walking in circles or meeting their classmates, more than one student greeted his neighbor with an occasional growl or lunge.

As we used to say when growing up, "No plan is perfect."

Judging from the efforts of the owners, it appeared that socialization took time and a tight grip on the leash.

The pups were put through the basic commands: sit, down, and stay with varying degrees of success.

Maybe, we concluded, the "monkey see, monkey do" philosophy was being employed. I mean after all, if you were a dog and everyone else around you was a dog, wouldn't you want to follow the leader's example?

The class lasted an hour, more than enough time to satisfy the anxious owners that they weren't alone in the training process, but rather were all in this battle for control together!

Before the class was over, we were hooked. We signed Sabrina up for the next class, one that began in two weeks. We could hardly wait.

Two Saturdays later, we watched as Sabrina eagerly jumped into the back seat of the car, obviously thinking she was off to the DQ. Wrong. Her first day of school was about to begin. Before long we would own the perfect canine.

We got to the store a few minutes early and watched as one by one Sabrina's classmates arrived. Her class included purebreds and mixed breeds in assorted sizes and shapes, with Sabrina being among the largest and most tolerant.

There were more than a few barks, growls, and lunges as the new classmates attempted group socialization for the first time.

Sabrina stood patiently next to me and looked over her new classmates, no doubt thinking, *"Oh, be quiet — some class. None of them even look like me."*

She was right on that count. Most of her new mates were of the small and fluffy variety, with only one Dalmatian equal to her in size.

Ever the lady, my little girl took all the barking, growling, and yapping in stride, ignoring the implied threats and words that if translated might not have been fit for polite company.

Her instructor appeared right on time. You could tell that he was itching to whip his new charges into shape.

The first order of business was roll call. All were present.

Next, the anxious parents were told to make a choice. One of us had to serve as the training partner.

Individuals with dogs obviously knew where they stood.

As for the rest of us, in most instances the men stepped forward, myself included. After all, according to Carla, Sabrina was "my" dog.

All of us took the reins with fear of the unknown causing a bit of a tingle in our stomachs. For the next hour we walked, we sat, and we walked again. We held on tightly to our leashes, repeatedly looked at our watches and prayed for the class to end.

We separated our pups when necessary, apologizing to each other. I'm sure that all of us were hoping against hope that at some point during the next five lessons the task of trainer's helper would become easier.

At the end of the lesson the instructor, hoping to rebuild our shattered confidence and no doubt ensure the fact that all of us would return for the second lesson, praised our effort and reminded us that success was a matter of trial and error, with error being the key word.

Our marching orders were simple: practice, practice, practice.

As we headed out the door and toward our car, chances were Sabrina was thinking, "*Well, that was easy. School's out, so it must be spring break.*"

With each week that passed, Sabrina seemed to gain more confidence. Commands in class were responded to quickly, and when the class was told to sit and pay attention, wonder of wonders, Sabrina did just that.

There was only one thing wrong with this picture. When we practiced at home, Sabrina's attention span was still in puppy mode. Moments after leaving class and both during and after practice at home, she reverted back to her loveable self.

We couldn't get mad at her. When we did, she'd just roll over on her back and with feet up in the air, submit.

She knew full well that within seconds her milk toast parents, father in particular, would be down on the floor rubbing her belly and telling her how wonderful she was.

We discussed our problem with her instructor and elicited two responses. The first, as expected, was practice, practice, practice.

Tell us something we don't already know, we thought. The second, "She's a very smart pup, you just have to grit your teeth, be patient, and remember that one day she'll wake up an adult and respond accordingly."

From God's lips to her beautiful head and pointed ears, we thought.

So there you have it, sports fans. Six weeks of lessons were about to come to an end.

We knew the makings of a PhD was living somewhere between those beautiful ears, all we had to do was wait, wait, wait, and of course practice, practice, practice.

With the ceremony over and the words *practice* ringing in our ears, we packed up our child and headed for a graduation treat, a large bowl of frozen custard at the DQ. School was out, but her home study program was about to begin in earnest.

What seemed like every day, but probably wasn't, Sabrina and I practiced in the front yard. With over an acre of ground to practice on and no distractions other than the local flora and fauna you'd think the setting was ideal. Apparently not!

I commanded her to come, sit, and stay until those words were indelibly etched in my brain, but unfortunately, that was the wrong brain.

How did I know this?

Well, when Carla called me to "come" to the table for dinner, I was there in a flash — Johnnie on the spot.

And when she told me to "sit" and "stay" at the table until our guests were through eating, you can bet I "sat" and didn't move a muscle until everyone was ready to leave the table.

Where had all of the training gone? Had weeks of near daily practice sessions gone to waste? They were obviously only benefiting one of us — me!

Was I frustrated? At times. Sabrina was so smart when she was in front of her classmates. She was even smart when we were practicing — sometimes! Then, suddenly, it was as if my little scholar had been hit by lightning and transformed into — who knows what. The puppy in her would rise to the surface and I might as well have been commanding a wall.

I was beginning to wonder if MY German shepherd was anything like the dogs I had read so much about before Sabrina came in to my life. Would she ever grow up? Did I really want to change her into a robot, or was there some way to bring out the best in her without ruining her playful and at times, devil may care attitude?

Boot Camp

Never giving up hope, and being good soldiers, Sabrina and I marched on.

However, I have to admit that time and practice, practice, practice doesn't always solve a communication problem, no matter how hard you try.

Looking back on our pet store schooling effort, I can safely say that from a socialization standpoint the trips to school helped.

Obedience training on the other hand was more illusion than fact. When you get right down to it, how much can you expect from your pet when you're working in an eight to ten foot circle — a circle filled with dogs of varying sizes, all barking, growling, and attempting to learn? In this kind of environment the chance of much information sinking in is suspect at best.

Was it a mistake to try? Of course not! Every experience in life brings you a little closer to your goal — assuming you and your pup are working off the same page.

But for real success, as you will see, nothing can match one-on-one training with a hardened and tested instructor.

Eventually, I found myself searching for another solution to training. This time it came in the form of an ad: "Leave your dog with us for a few weeks, and before you know it I'll return it to you a changed and 'happy camper." Well, at least we didn't have to drive to upstate New York to leave her with the monks at the New Skete Monistary.

The ad sounded too good to be true, and when anything sounds too good to be true — well, you got it.

I called, talked, listened, and asked for references. I checked several and found that with each call I was talking to a satisfied dog owner. As it turned out, they must have been relatives!

Carla and I talked it over. We agreed that we weren't making much progress. So with love in our hearts, we packed up some of Sabrina's toys, an ample supply of dog food, and sent the love of our life off to doggy camp.

The only thing that changed with her absence was the fact that we realized how much we missed her. It was only a couple of weeks, but it seemed like forever!

Two weeks later her trainer proudly showed off the new Sabrina. We were impressed. Was this the same pup we'd left in the hands of this stranger a few weeks ago?

As far as Sabrina was concerned, chances are she had concluded, "*I better make this look good, or they'll leave me here forever!*"

When I took over the leash, she was all licks and tail wags. I don't know who was more excited, her or me. Had she spoken English I'm sure she would have promised to be good for the rest of her life.

After watching her work with the trainer, we began to believe that her two-week trip might have been the answer.

Then it was my turn, and Sabrina responded to my every command.

As far as her promise of a lifetime of goodness was concerned, that wasn't really necessary. From the day she entered our lives, save for the experience in Carla's car, and her flight of fancy with a feather pillow, she was a perfect pup. As far as we were concerned, we were in this training "thing" together!

We sat with the trainer and went over future training procedures and the enforcement of rules.

Her advice to us brought back memories of lessons past.

Wonder what she said ? You guessed it — practice, practice, practice!

Of course, once home and among family and friends, Sabrina reverted back to the Sabrina of old.

I have to admit, I was beside myself. To say I was dumbfounded was an understatement. I was beginning to wonder if dogs, like humans, suffered from attention deficit disorder. The love of my life had four left feet, and all of them seemed to be tangled in her leash at the same time.

Face it. I don't know a pet owner that doesn't believe that his or her pet is the most beautiful, smartest, four-legged creature ever created.

Carla and I fell into this category. After all, wasn't Rin Tin Tin a German shepherd? So, wasn't it safe to assume that Sabrina was as brilliant as she was beautiful?

I thought so!

As far as Sabrina and more training was concerned, by now she had probably concluded, "*Go ahead, find another trainer. I've got this training thing all figured out.*"

Did we give up on our beautiful girl? Absolutely not! Hardly a day went by that didn't see us out in the front yard practicing.

For that matter, hardly a day went by that didn't find me trying to find a new solution to our training problem.

I don't know why we didn't think of it earlier, but suddenly I heard, "Let your fingers do the walking," and mine did, straight to the Yellow Pages.

Under dog training we found an ad for a Schutzhund school. I had no idea what that meant, but the ad stated that they trained dogs for police, drug sniffing, and other specialized work.

To me that meant German shepherds, so I called ahead and made an appointment to meet the head trainer. This time, we drove fifty miles in search of perfection.

Never, say "never!"

The training facility wasn't like anything we'd ever seen before. The school was a ten-acre tract, all fenced.

Waiting for us was the head instructor, Debbie. One look at her, she was tiny, and you could picture the German shepherds walking all over her.

She described the school and the buildings of varying sizes that served as hiding places during training.

As we walked with Debbie she pointed out that dogs and their handlers were sent out along with a instructor to search for and secure a villain.

Let me tell you, although the villains were well padded and never hurt, I'm not sure I'd want to be found by seventy-five pounds of snarling German shepherd.

The grounds were also used for "track and find" drills. Debbie explained that trainers would hide a package, and then the handler-trainee would release his dog with orders to track and find. The dogs were allotted so much time, and time and time again they would mark the spot, then retrieve the package, and return to their handlers, all smiles and tails wagging.

There were fences of varying sizes, and other forms of obstacles for agility training purposes. It didn't take much to convince me that this was hard core, serious training, as we watched several dogs being put through their paces. It was really something to see.

Debbie explained everything that we were watching in detail. Finally, it appeared we had found someone that might know how to bring out the best in our child.

On the other hand, if I was a dog I'd probably be covering my eyes and hoping that this was all a bad dream.

As usual, Sabrina took the idea of more training in stride. "*Another pushover. Piece a cake. I'll do my puppy thing, and before she knows it this trainer will be mine!*"

We told Debbie that we weren't interested in Sabrina for protection. Our sole purpose was obedience training. We pointed out that she was a lover, not a fighter and we wanted her to stay that way!

I explained that she'd been through two training programs and how each time — although she performed admirably in school — once home, school was out.

Unbeknown to us, Debbie had been watching Sabrina all the while we were walking and watching the training that was underway.

"She's just a puppy, isn't she?" she asked. "She probably won't grow out of the puppy stage for another couple of years."

As she could tell from the look on our faces, that wasn't what we needed to hear. We were mortified!

"That's all right," she said. "This is the perfect time to train her properly."

"*Sabrina," I said to myself, "I hope you're listening?*""

We breathed a sigh of relief. There was still hope. Could it be true — could we have finally found Nirvana?

Debbie asked which of us would serve as assistant trainer, and as usual, Carla made it abundantly clear that Sabrina was my dog and that I would be working with her.

Once the assistant issue was decided Debbie explained, "I'll want Sabrina for six to ten one-hour private sessions. We'll conduct all of the training here."

"The sessions will be every other week, and in between each class I'll expect you to practice, and then practice some more!"

There were those words again!

Yes sir, er, ma'am, I thought, meaning no disrespect.

If it wasn't for the difference in facilities, I was beginning to think that all trainers graduated from the same school. What separated this instructor from the others was the fact that although she was only about five foot two, Debbie reminded me of a marine drill instructor. Hands on her hips. Back ramrod straight. Feet spread apart. Eyes focused directly on me, and leaving little doubt as to the chain of command!

With the training schedule established, we began making the one-hundred-mile round trip on alternating Saturday mornings.

The first session proved to be more of a get acquainted hour for the instructor and Sabrina than one involving Sabrina and I. I watched as Debbie began a training process that I was sure would transform my child in to a full-fledged, and most important, obedient German shepherd.

In a matter of minutes Sabrina found out who was driving the bus, and it wasn't her. From then on, Debbie had her total and undivided attention!

As Carla and I watched Debbie work with Sabrina that first day we were amazed. This couldn't be the same little girl we knew and loved. Look at the way she moved. Look at her head and the smile on her face.

Our loveable child must have thought she'd been drafted. I could hear her thinking, *"This isn't good. Left, right, left, right. Turn. Stop. She means business."*

The harder Debbie pushed Sabrina, the more she actually appeared to like it. She was attentive, and her tail never stopped wagging.

You should have seen her looking up at Debbie as they moved across the field. They were moving as one, and I was envious!

Carla brought our camcorder and while the camera was running I repeatedly heard, "See? See? Look how she pays attention. You're going to have to be firm with her.

Remember, you're the boss, the pack leader — do it just like Debbie!"

There's nothing like a supportive wife at times like this!

Finally, toward the end of that first training session I got a chance to try my hand and was promptly told in no uncertain terms, that I *was* the pack leader, the boss, king of the hill, and I had to start acting like it.

Our trips to "Boot Camp" and the practice that followed reminded me of a slogan, "send us your son and we'll return him a man. Army, Strong!

Sabrina hadn't enlisted when she began Shutzhund obedience training. She entered a loveable, adult puppy, no doubt thinking that once again she would pull the wool over her parent's as well as her instructors' eyes. Not this time. Several weeks and whimpers later she would still be my fun-loving adult puppy. Some things never change. However, now she would respond to my commands instantly.

I was still her dotting, Casper-milk-toast father, always worrying that the next snap of the leash or strong command would damage my little girl's psyche. Yet, somewhere along the way Sergeant Debbie's demand that I, "man up, she's not made of glass — you lead and she responds" would change me as well. Slowly but surely I would become the "top dog, the alpha male!"

"Don't ask Sabrina to do something," Debbie barked, "Shout it out — say it like you mean it!"

Shouting out orders to my little girl wasn't easy. However, it was either that, or come face to face with Sergeant Debbie!

Suddenly, Sabrina began to respond happily and immediately to my every command. I was beginning to get with the program — leaders lead and puppies followed!

But that is my little girl out there on the end of that leash, I thought. *How can I be mean to her?*

"I know what you're thinking," Debbie barked.

How could she? I was just in the process of thinking it. But she was right. I was told to keep a firm grip on the reins — to command and expect results!

She told me that I would know when the two of us had achieved "oneness." "When you are moving together, with Sabrina off your left hip, looking up at you and smiling as she awaits your every move and command, — that's "oneness."

"When you begin to move together — that is when you will have become a team, rather than just another per owner, allowing his dog to take him for a walk!"

Was she dreaming?

Slowly, but surely, I was beginning to believe that my dream of attaining this lofty goal, with Sabrina by my side, might just become a reality!

I could hardly wait to achieve the end result — but wait I did.

However, Sergeant Debbie didn't. At the end of our first lesson she showed Carla and I a pinch collar and told us that she would bring one in the proper size to Sabrina's next lesson.

I took one look at the prongs on that collar and cringed. How could I inflict such pain on my little love?

You should have seen the look that collar got from Sabrina. *Hey! Remember me? I'm your favorite little girl. You can't use that thing on me; you'll make me cry.*

Once again, Debbie was reading my mind, or maybe all pet owners responded the same way. "It won't hurt her. It will serve to keep her focused. It's a training tool, not a punishment or reprimand," Debbie announced.

Well, like everything that was thrown at her, Sabrina took to the pinch collar with a smile on her face, pep in her step, and her tail wagging. Yes, there was the occasional yelp when the pinch really pinched, but for the most part she got the message and began to respond accordingly.

Our lessons consisted of running, walking, and jogging with a variety of turns, sudden stops, and starts thrown in, in order to throw my girl off stride.

While in the midst of one or the other of these actions Debbie would shout out, "Turn left. Turn right. Stop and quickly turn and come back toward me."

Sabrina was expected to stay at the heel position, just off my left hip. And, as time went on, she began to do just that.

When the command to "heel" was given, it was usually followed by, sit, down, and stay.

Once in the down position, Sabrina learned to stay in place as I either walked away, over or around her. The objective: she was to remain in the down-stay position no matter what I or anyone else did.

At first she was up and ready with a lick, but after a while nothing would move her short of a command from me to either sit or come.

Control, I could feel it. I was actually becoming the pack leader. Slowly but surely I was beginning to take charge!

Her training started out in the winter and ended in early summer.

Unlike her father, Sabrina loved cold weather. If there was snow on the ground she was like a kid with a new toy. She would run around and suddenly flop down and roll in it. When she wasn't rolling around in it, she would bury her nose in it. Upon finding her nose coated with ice, she would shake her head from side to side in order to get rid of it. If that didn't work, her tongue would come out, as she tried to lick it off.

What a sight!

During our months of training together, the two of us slowly but surely attained the oneness that Debbie had promised.

My little girl took to obedience training under the watchful eye and, when needed, strong right arm of Sergeant Debbie and I. She was happy as a clam. Nothing could wipe the constant smile of her face.

Nothing and no one would ever break her spirit!

Each lesson would begin in the same way. Before learning something new, Debbie would put us through our paces, shouting commands and expecting perfection.

If Sabrina wore boots, I'm sure she would have been required to spit shine them and stand for inspection before each lesson.

It was while we were working our way through the course that we discovered that Sabrina had a stomach problem. She was lactose intolerant. This put an end to DQ rewards. I, in turn, tried to make up for this loss by carrying plenty of dog biscuits and other treats with me.

Carla continued to tape each lesson. Then, between lessons the three of us would sit in front of the TV and review and critique our latest performance.

Ham that she was, Sabrina's ears would perk up as she sat smiling and watching, no doubt thinking, *"Hey, look me over. I'm a star"!*

I am sure that Sabrina thought being on television was pretty cool until she realized that she was the one doing all the work.

Carla seldom let up on me. As far as she was concerned, I was a wimp when it came to being stern with my baby. But as time went on, I began to show signs of progress, albeit with my wimpy side carefully hidden.

In between lessons I would take Sabrina to a college campus five miles from home. They had plenty of grass for training, and in between stops by an occasional student or professor to watch and meet Sabrina, the two of us would practice, practice, practice using a forty-foot leash.

Over time, my big girl built up quite a campus following. The more people watched, the more she seemed to enjoy showing off her newly learned skills. She was all ham!

She'd always been frightened by the sound of cars and trucks, so I made it a point to work her on a large grassy area that fronted a major highway. At first she was hesitant, but as time went on her fear was replaced by a solid performance when in the "stay" position. We were becoming a team — she trusted me!

Little by little, my little girl — to me she was always a little girl — was coming of age. Maybe she'd be a puppy for a few more years, but she'd be a well-trained and obedient one. Yep. My little girl was growing up.

More training rather than less was a good thing. With every lesson, Sabrina was exposed to more information. She may not have known it at the time, but I really believe that each training program we tried built a foundation for the success she ultimately achieved at that Schutzhund Center.

During the course of her training, something else was taking place that would mark a major change for all of us.

My overseas consulting project had expanded, and I found myself making trips to Florida to meet with a firm that my employers were interested in doing business with.

With each trip, I came home wishing that our weather and water were equal to that of what I was seeing.

We had a sailboat, but because the Cumberland River, which ran behind our house, was too narrow for sailing, it stayed on its trailer.

Bass boats and pontoon boats were the boats of choice. In fact, when we finally decided to rent dock space at a marina nearby and put *Solitude* in the water, you would have thought we were Mr. and Mrs. Christopher Columbus.

"Ain't never had one a them 'round here," the marina manager noted. "Mind puttin' the sails up and letting me take a picture fer our bulletin board?"

If you think that was an odd request, you should've seen two of my neighbors and me attempting to step the mast. It was the blind leading the blind, but believe it or not, the blind prevailed!

During our first and last attempt to go sailing, we found that, the Cumberland River never seemed to get wide enough to set the sails. As we were motoring back to our dock in the marina, our ever reliable motor blew up. Now, we were, as some say, '*up a creek without a paddle.*'

I got on the radio and tried to reach the park ranger station that I knew was in the area. As it turned out, he didn't keep his radio on the channel I was using. So we sat — and sat. Then along came some folks in a powerboat. We flagged them down. They agreed to tow us back to our marina, so we tossed them a line and off we went. Trust me, there is nothing more humiliating for a "sailor" than to be seen on the wrong end of a tow line. This highlight marked the end our desire to sail.

Well, getting back to my travels, I came home from one of my trips to Florida and told Carla, "We're moving."

"We're what?"

"Moving, I want sunshine, blue skies and water, lots of water to sail on," I responded.

Well, we already owned a home in Cape Coral, Florida, that we'd purchased years earlier, intending to live there part time after I retired. The house was on a wide canal with a dock and direct access to the Gulf of Mexico.

Over the years we used it as a rental. In between renters we'd knocked out walls, replaced cabinets, and made all of the changes we thought we'd like when we were ready to begin spending our winters in Florida.

Having made my decision, we boarded Sabrina, and Carla and I took a quick trip to Cape Coral, Florida, to inspect our house. The renters had just moved out, so we had it all to ourselves.

One look at the eight-foot ceilings was all it took to convince us that no matter how many changes we had made since purchasing the house, we'd never be happy — it was just too closed in.

We'd owned a very contemporary house in Texas before I retired, with soaring ceilings and skylights. I guess that open feeling coupled with the eighteen to over twenty-foot ceilings in our Tennessee house had spoiled us.

If this collection of homes sounds confusing, it really isn't. At one point we owned two homes for retirement purposes and a home in Texas where our company was headquartered.

With the Texas house already sold, we selected a realtor and put the Florida house on the market. When we returned to Gallatin, our pup must have thought we'd given her away. She was beside herself the minute she saw us, tail wagging, bouncing up and down, crying, and carrying on.

Over the next several weeks we talked and talked about Florida. Once again, it was a good thing Sabrina's vocabulary was limited.

Carla wasn't enthused about making a move, and I was finally told, "If you want to move, go find us a house." At which point she outlined what she wanted in the way of new surroundings and made it clear that she had no intention of joining the hunt.

I already knew what I wanted. We couldn't have a swimming pool at our current house, the ground was solid rock, and the spa we'd installed on our deck overlooking the river just wasn't a pool.

Even if we could have sailed where we were living, having a dock on the Cumberland River had been out of the question because the Corp of Engineers said that the river's current and wash from barge traffic on the river would rip it out. I tried to fight them, but it didn't take long for me to learn that when it came to the river it was their way or no way.

It should come as no surprise that my short list where a house in Florida was concerned included a dock for the boat and a pool. No big deal! Carla's list included higher ceilings, a suitable room for the cats, of course, and room outdoors for her to create raised beds for her gardening. And oh, yes, a clear night sky for her telescope.

Try as I might, Carla wouldn't budge and go with me to Florida to look. So I did my research on the Internet, lined up realtors, and armed with our camcorder, got on a plane and flew to Fort Myers, Florida.

"You want a house? I'll find you, me, Sabrina, and the cats a house. Just watch," I said as I departed for the airport.

I looked at homes in Cape Coral and decided our once small town had become a city and was far too crowded. After living amid peace and quiet, there were just too many people and too much traffic. What's more, they were constructing office buildings, shopping malls, and strip centers on every available piece of land.

For reasons I can't remember, I wandered north to a small city called Punta Gorda. You may have heard of it thanks to Hurricane Charley. It's an all waterfront community jutting into Charlotte Harbor, which in turn, leads to the Gulf of Mexico. In the nineties "Money "magazine had listed Punta Gorda as one of the best waterfront and boating communities in the country.

The first couple of brokers I visited told me I couldn't possibly find a home in the price range I wanted. As far as they were concerned, Punta Gorda had a reputation to maintain and it came at a price!

Tell me something can't be done, and I'll work twice as hard to prove that it can.

I met a couple of women at a Century 21 office in Port Charlotte, about thirty miles north of our Cape Coral house, and lo and behold, they found just what I believed we wanted. It was a little more than I had intended to spend, but the final decision rested with Carla.

We'd owned three homes when I retired, and I'd made up my mind that at this time in our lives we only needed so much space and one home would do just fine.

Our Dallas house sold within days of going on the market. This was quite a surprise, as our brokers had told us that being a contemporary design in a traditional market, we'd be very lucky if it sold in three months. Not only did they prove to be wrong, we found ourselves faced with buyers that wanted a quick close.

The Cape Coral house was on the market, and, being waterfront property, we expected it to go quickly as well. So in a way, we were already in the process of downsizing.

My house hunting completed, I flew home. I had several houses on video tape for Carla to review.

As it turned out, we both liked the most expensive one — the one in Punta Gorda.

We negotiated back and forth with the owner and finally brought the price down to one we could live with. I promised the owner a quick close, one within two weeks. He accepted, and with the help of the gals from Century 21, we moved ahead to do just that.

Why am I talking about house hunting when this is a story about a dog?

Well, once again, if Sabrina understood what we were planning she would no doubt have stated, quite emphatically, "*Hey, remember me, the dog? No one asked me where I want to live. Do they have pigs and goats and deer and — I don't think I'm gonna like this!*

What did our moving to Florida have to do with Sabrina?

More than we could have imagined!

Sabrina's Move from Hell

Sabrina loved riding in the car. Of course, the fact that I'd taken her everywhere with me ever since she was a pup didn't hurt. As a result, with the house sold, I figured our three-day trip to Florida would be one big joyride for the both of us.

Instead, I was about to find out that you can never take anything for granted. During the next two weeks I would discover my inner self and unlock feelings, fears, and a level of love that I thought I possessed but had obviously been buried deep within me!

Ask a roomful of people to define *love*, and I guarantee you will get a roomful of answers.

"It's that warm and fuzzy feeling that leaves you weak in the knees."

"Well, you know, you really can't define it. You just know it."

"It's when sparks fly, like watching fireworks. You feel it all over."

No matter how you define it, all I can tell you is that for me, our move from Tennessee to Florida and the days that followed taught me that love was more than a word, a hug, or a kiss.

Don't get me wrong. I love my wife. She's my lover, my best friend, and the most caring individual I've ever known. So why did I find myself asking, *How could a dog, a pet, transform me into a better, more caring, and loving person than I thought I was?*

The morning of Sabrina's trip from hell began with the movers showing up late. This was not a good sign, but we weren't in any hurry — we were retired!

Minutes after they arrived at the top of our hill, everything came to a halt. The driver and his partner stood looking down at the road leading to our house. Hands on their hips they tried to figure out how best to navigate down the hill and close to our front door — backwards.

After a brief conference, the driver took one shot at backing his eighteen-wheeler down the hill, and then threw in the towel. He marched down the hill and told us it was impossible to maneuver his sixty-foot tractor-trailer to a point just off our carport for loading.

We talked him into trying again, and after a few more half-hearted attempts he made it abundantly clear that he and his partner had no intention of lugging the contents of our house up the hill.

The driver suggested they return with two smaller trucks. They would load and later reload our belongings into the larger truck back at their yard. Having been through more than one horror story with movers we refused their offer.

Our next door neighbor Steve had been watching and offered to help. He described his over-the-road driving credentials to the driver, and the driver told him, "Take your best shot." Steve got behind the wheel, and before you could say, "Put her here," made the task of positioning that big rig look like child's play.

Nine hours later we were loaded, and the movers were on their way up the hill and headed for the highway. We were to meet them at our new home in a week.

By now, it was too late to get on the road. So the cats, Carla, Sabrina, and I returned to a house that echoed with emptiness.

The cats, already in carriers, were returned to their empty room. Sabrina, Carla, and I stretched out on the floor in the master bedroom, hoping to get some sleep.

Cats don't seem to care where you take them as long as there's a clean litter box, plenty of water, and their meals are delivered promptly. As far as our felines were concerned nothing had changed. They would sleep soundly and be bright eyed and bushy tailed, ready to hit the road in the morning.

Sabrina, on the other hand, had seen enough. Our first warning that something was wrong should have been her failure to eat much of her food during the day, but then she'd always been a finicky eater. We figured this was just our spoiled brat's way of putting her paws down.

"Take me away from my friends will you? I'll show you. I'll go on a hunger strike!"

She spent the night wandering the empty rooms crying. We talked to her. Petted, rubbed, and tried to console her. Nothing seemed to work. By morning she'd vomited several times and had a good case of diarrhea.

Not wanting to leave until her discomfort and failure to eat was sorted out, we called our vet. He thought we'd left town, but upon hearing our problem, agreed to see us immediately.

After checking Sabrina he pronounced her condition a tummy ache brought on by the stress of watching her house emptied out. Oh, really! You think?

"Nothing to worry about," he said. "You know how anxious she can get when anything around her changes. She'll be just fine before you know it."

With that diagnosis came the typical "Take two aspirin and call me" line that doctors seem to use when they don't know what's going on.

He gave us some medicine to settle Sabrina's stomach, handed us a bill, and wished us well on the trip and move.

At last all systems were "go," or so we'd been assured. We were about to hit the road.

Carla would take the cats and assorted larger boxes in her minivan.

Our twenty-four-foot sailboat would be towed behind the van, as she had a vehicle with the power to pull the load. We hoped.

Sabrina and whatever couldn't be carried in the van would go with me. Small boxes were stacked on the floor and front seat. Larger ones, along with our luggage went in the trunk.

Sabrina required full use of the backseat, which turned out to be a wise move.

Because we were towing our sailboat we'd decided to take a longer, flatter route to Florida. It was summer, and we had no idea how Carla's van would handle the heat and extra load.

It didn't take long to find out. Once into the first hills in Alabama, Carla's voice came over my radio. "My temperature gauge is way up, it's in the red."

We pulled to the side of the highway for a discussion and concluded that when approaching an area of hills she should turn off the air conditioning and open her windows for ventilation. Once out of the hills she could turn the air conditioning back on.

This became standard operating procedure for several hundred miles. It wasn't fun, but at least she and the cats had air conditioning throughout most of the trip.

Next, it was my turn to stop. Not long after we'd pulled over to solve Carla's cooling dilemma, we were faced with a new one.

I heard the unmistakable sound of a pending vomit behind me. One look in the rear view mirror, and I could see Sabrina's head bobbing up and down. I immediately hit my turn signal and began looking for a spot where Carla and I could pull off the highway.

Fortunately, Sabrina held on 'til I could get off the road and around to the opposite side of the car to let her out. Once out, up came the last of what little food she'd eaten in the past twenty-four hours.

Hoping this was just an adverse reaction to the medicine the vet had given her, we got back on the road. For a while, everything was fine; then, there was that sound again.

We pulled off and repeated our last stop. Fortunately, Sabrina was again able to hold on until I could get her out of the car.

Now Carla and I were beginning to worry. During the next several hours we pulled off the road a number of times to allow Sabrina to fight her way through what had become a bout of the dry heaves.

We tried to get her to take a little water fearing she would become dehydrated. She showed little interest and with each stop our concerns grew. The initial part of the trip was taking us through farm country and small towns, affording us no chance to find a vet.

I know this will sound strange when you read it, and I'll probably mention it again, but believe it or not, whenever Sabrina was hurting, I could feel her pain. I know this sounds silly, but so help me it's true.

By the time we were off the road and in a motel for the night, Sabrina's stomach seemed to have settled down.

It was late, and as fate would have it, we were in a small town in Alabama, so finding an emergency clinic or vet was out of the question.

I'm pretty sure I slept with one eye open, fearing the worst, but surprisingly the night was incident free. After a quick breakfast at the motel, we rounded up our charges and began day two of our journey.

Sabrina ate very little, but we assumed this was because of her upset stomach and medication. All we could do was hope that with a night's rest and a little food and water she would begin to return to her old self.

Once out of the room, my little girl seemed to have perked up as she hauled me to the back door of "her" car. With a smile on her face and her tail sweeping back and forth, she waited patiently for me to drop the luggage I was carrying and open her door. Once open, she leaped in and took up her position as chief observer and designated backseat driver. Things appeared to be looking up.

We checked the boat and trailer to make certain everything was as we'd left it.

Checked tire pressures and pronounced ourselves ready to travel.

It didn't take long for Sabrina to begin a repeat performance of day one. During the course of our second day we made several stops to allow her to walk around, drink water, and settle down.

We checked our map and agreed to pull off the road for the night in Lake City, Florida, a town large enough to have a Wal-Mart Super Center and several vets.

Carla was concerned that Sabrina's limited liquid intake over the past two days would lead to dehydration, so our first stop after checking into a motel was the Wal-Mart Center where we picked up several bottles of Pedialyte.

The next morning we found a vet and took her in for a checkup. We showed him the paperwork from our vet back home and advised him that we were on our way to our new home and expected to arrive late in the day.

After checking Sabrina thoroughly, he concluded that anxiety or a stomach virus was the cause of her problem. We were given new meds to settle her stomach and told we were good to go."

By now I was experiencing a sensation that, unbeknown to me, would return many times over the next nine years. I wasn't just concerned; I was scared. Our vet had said everything would be fine, but so far he was wrong. And we were about to see how vet number two faired.

His solution was no better than his predecessor. Every couple of hours found us stopped along the side of the road or at a rest area.

We arrived at our new home in Punta Gorda late in the evening and seeing another empty house didn't help Sabrina's stomach. The smile was there, but by now she was weak, lethargic, and unwilling to even look at food or water.

By midnight we bundled her in the car and headed to neighboring Port Charlotte and a vet emergency clinic that was open 'round the clock.

I guess all vets have a standard operating procedure. Vet number three followed the path of vets one and two. She felt around, poked, probed, and explored.

She consulted her assistant. They shook their heads, decided to take X-rays, and conducted more inspections.

When vet number three was through, she suggested we leave Sabrina with her for the night. She wanted to re-hydrate and feed her intravenously and monitor her response. This didn't help my disposition, but at two in the morning her recommendation seemed logical.

Later that morning, after checking on Sabrina, we began asking around in an effort to find a permanent vet with good credentials just in case.

We picked Sabrina up at the emergency clinic mid afternoon and armed with her ever expanding medical records and new meds, headed for home.

Forty-eight hours later we were at vet number four, a vet that had come highly recommended by one of our new neighbors.

He reviewed the stack of vet reports we'd collected on the trip and having completed his own examination, suggested we leave Sabrina with him for several days.

By now, she was extremely weak, and he wanted time to run more tests and try to build her strength back using intravenous meds, food, and fluids.

There is nothing more heartbreaking than trying to respond to a small child or your pet when they're sick. They're unable to communicate, so you place your faith in the hands of doctors and God.

The look on Sabrina's face as the vet took her from us said it all. *Hey, Dad, I'll be good. I promise. I may feel sick as a dog, but if you take me home I'll be good.* Her tail was down. Her ears were down, and her father was suffering from a broken heart.

Several doctors and even more prescriptions had come and gone. My heart was breaking, yet all I could do was wait and hope.

So far we'd seen four vets, piled up more than a thousand dollars in vet bills and nobody could answer a simple question, "What was wrong with my little girl?"

My concerns had nothing to do with money. Sabrina was a member of our family. I wanted answers and a satisfactory resolution.

She spent nearly a week as a guest of vet number four. Carla and I made daily visits in an effort to cheer her up, and no matter how bad she might have felt inside, the moment she saw us she was, well, Sabrina. All smiles!

Finally, we were told we could take her home, and once again we left with those famous last words ringing in our ears, "Here are her new meds. Don't worry she's going to be just fine."

Our house was beginning to look like a home by the time Sabrina stepped through the door again, which probably helped, but not very much. She was fine for a few days, but that didn't last. Once again, her stomach problems and lack of interest in food returned.

Believe it or not, we decided to try another vet. This one, Dr. Andrea Bivens, did what none of the others had done. Yes, she went over Sabrina's now voluminous recent medical history and checked her thoroughly. However, when she was done, she told us, "I'm not sure what's causing the problem. I'd like you to take her to see a specialist in Sarasota. It's about fifty miles away." She wanted Sabrina to be seen by Dr. Heidi Ward, an internal medicine and oncology specialist.

On one hand, this response was like a gift from God. Maybe, just maybe, we'd finally found our new veterinarian. After all, she was the only vet willing to step forward or maybe back, and say, "I just don't know."

Until now, I had no idea that pet specialists existed. However, at this point, feeling totally helpless, I was willing to reach out to anyone that could help us!

Because of Carla's experience with dogs and cats, she made the call to discuss medical issues. Dr. Ward listened as she described the past few weeks and Dr. Bivens's recommendation and told her to bring Sabrina to Sarasota immediately.

I hadn't slept well for several nights thinking about my little girl. Now thinking about the word *oncologist* launched me over the edge. I knew what oncologists did, and all I could see was the possibility of losing Sabrina. No matter how I tried, I couldn't erase that thought from my mind as we drove to Sarasota.

I think it was at this point that my relationship with Sabrina changed. I'm not sure why, but for some reason, I'd blocked out the word *internist*. During that drive, God began to teach me the real meaning of caring and just how deeply I could love. Mentally, I was beginning to come unhinged, all I kept visualizing was the word "oncologist!"

From the day she came into our lives, Sabrina loved everyone. She wouldn't hurt a flea. Vets could tie her in knots, poke and prod her, and she would just lie on the examining table with a smile on her face. What was happening just didn't seem fair!

Everyone has moments in their life that they will never forget. This was one of mine. I felt as though God was testing all of us.

We didn't know it at the time, but this was just the first of what would be many trips we would make to see Dr. Ward. It was a drive made in silence. Carla drove, and I was left with my thoughts, thinking the worst and praying for the best.

With everything we'd been through these past few weeks, I've often wondered how many pet owners would have concluded, "Enough already- time to send her away and begin looking for a new dog."

That thought never entered my mind.

From the first time I held my oversized, nine-week-old fuzz-ball, she touched me in ways that even now I find difficult to express.

As I looked into her big brown eyes, eyes that were able to melt my heart, I vowed I would never allow her to remain in pain needlessly and that no matter what, I would see to it that she was given every opportunity to spend a long life with us.

I've never been an overly religious person. Yet I've always believed there is a God and that he's up there, somewhere, listening to all of us when we need him.

I seldom asked for anything for myself, always for others, and this time was no different.

While Sabrina was a guest of vet number four I found myself asking God to look after and take good care of her. I didn't know it at the time, but that request would be repeated over and over again throughout our relationship.

From the day she came to live with us, no day ended without my getting down on the floor to stroke and tell her to, "Have good doggy dreams and dream of angels," because to me she was one.

Sabrina never went to sleep without a kiss on the head. No day ended without her knowing how special she was and how much she was loved.

She repaid Carla and I in kind with non-stop love, a constant desire to please, loyalty, and a fierce devotion that, until she became a member of our family, I never knew was possible in a pet.

During our years together, I would find myself telling her she couldn't die before me. I knew she didn't understand, but I told her anyway. I told her that I'd be waiting for her when she got to heaven, all the while knowing that was probably out of the question.

Were my feelings strange, unique to me? I don't think so. Whether they knew it or not, I'd be willing to bet that the same unconditional love Sabrina showered upon us and we on her was being experienced daily by pet owners throughout the world.

The fifty-mile drive to Sarasota seemed to last forever, but as it turned out it was well worth every minute and mile.

We liked Dr. Ward from the moment we met.

Maybe it was because she spent so much time dealing with death. Who's to say? But for whatever reason, watching her work with Sabrina we could feel the love she passed to her patients.

We didn't know it at the time, but Dr. Ward would become a member of our care giving family over the next nine years.

After completing a battery of blood tests, soundings, and X-rays, we finally had the answer to what had become a quest, our child had irritable bowel syndrome.

I had no idea what that meant, but I was sure it wasn't good - and it wasn't. But, there was a happy ending to this part of our story. As it turned out, it was treatable and to a large degree controllable.

For the rest of her life Sabrina would be subject to anxiety attacks brought on by any change in her environment. The attacks would trigger the response we'd experienced over the past two weeks. Over time, if Sabrina wasn't medicated and watched, the attacks could tear the lining of her stomach.

Dr. Ward spent a good deal of time explaining the problem, Sabrina's future care and the need for us to see that her environment was kept stable and as anxiety free as possible.

She put her on several new meds. One of them, prednisone, was a drug she would be on for the rest of her life.

We would need to bring her up to Sarasota for periodic checkups until Dr. Ward was satisfied that the meds and diet our child was going to begin were working.

That's right. Dogs go on diets too!

Prednisone was one of the last drugs I wanted to hear. I'd seen what it had done to my daughter Nanci, and I'd heard horror stories from others that had taken the drug for long periods of time.

I knew the drug well — knew that it worked. However, as with so many drugs today, the side effects were often worse than the cure. In Sabrina's case, even though she'd been put on a diet, her weight was about to balloon up from the mid seventies to one hundred and five pounds as a result of the prednisone. Other changes would be more subtle — noticed only by Carla and I.

The idea of trying to lose weight at the same time the prednisone was forcing it up seemed an impossible task. Somehow, we would have to manage Sabrina's weight while her meds worked overtime to force it higher!

Weight control was about to take on a whole new meaning for our girl. There would be no more treats, at least not as she knew them.

Imagine someone suddenly taking desserts and all of your favorite foods away from you. I was sure Sabrina's response, if she could talk, would have gone something like this: "*Did I hear Dr. Ward right? No more dog biscuits and chew treats? Veggies — forever! Yuk!*"

That's right. She'd already given up trips to the Dairy Queen and now, her favorite treats were about to be replaced by dehydrated and regular baby carrots and a variety of veggies with pills hidden in them.

We left Dr. Ward's office confident that Sabrina was finally on the road to recovery, albeit one that could crash at any time. Through it all, no matter how sick or how weak she'd been, her demeanor never changed. The smile was always there, and her tail never stopped moving.

Life with Sabrina turned out to be a constant challenge. We never knew when she was hurting. No matter how bad she felt or how much pain she was in, she treated every moment as if that was the way she was supposed to be and feel. It became our job to recognize when something was wrong!

Oh, in case you were wondering how the cats handled the move to their new address, very well, thank you very much.

They took to their new home as if they were born to live in Florida. They had a large, bright cattery, good food, and plenty of warm Florida sunshine whenever they stretched out in cat beds on the lanai.

You heard right. On any given day you could find the little rascals on the lanai, curled up in a pile on one or both of their cat beds. That, of course, was assuming that their evil stepsister had been placed in a "time out" in her crate.

Our cat kids loved the sunshine. As far as they were concerned, all was right with the world.

Just to add to our Florida welcome, during our first two months we were sideswiped by two hurricanes. No major damage occurred; although a portion of our lanai roof fell in as a result of the second storm.

This prompted those immortal words spoken to husbands the world over by their wives, "See? I told you so," followed in this case by, "That's what happens when you live in Florida!"

Carla immediately added to her list of Florida living requirements: "If you're forcing me to live here I want hurricane shutters before next season, or we're going back to Tennessee."

Asked for and ordered!

Sabrina, had she heard the preceding, would no doubt have added her two cents worth, "*Yeah, look what it's done to me!*"

Wondering about my little girl?

It's a good thing dogs live in the moment. After what seemed a lifetime to us, but was probably just another day in her life, God seemed to be smiling down on her.

Her new home was beginning to look and feel sort of like the house she'd left behind.

Dr. Wards diet, although not a feast for gourmets wasn't quite as bad as she thought.

Our little girl was beginning to make new friends and, had taken the time to carefully sniff and mark every blade of grass surrounding her house — as her private territory. Granted, there weren't any pigs or wild turkeys running around, but there were some strange looking birds with really long necks!

Like the cats, she'd discovered the lanai, the sun, and the empty cat beds. Before you can say, "Pass the suntan lotion," our little girl was on her way to becoming a Florida girl — sans bikini!

I've Got People to Meet, Places to Go, Things to Do

Well, I guess you could say that Carla, Sabrina, the cats, and I were officially Floridians. We'd experienced the outer edges of two hurricanes in a matter of forty-five days. During that time we'd seen the damage they could do up as close as we ever wanted to be, both at our house and on television.

We'd seen and experienced enough to know that we didn't want to meet the full force of a hurricane face to face.

Our new home was a little light on neighbors at the time of our move. There were only three homes on our street and a couple of homes across the canal from us.

Punta Gorda Isles is a canal community planned for approximately four thousand homes, and that was just fine with us. Our best guess at the time was that no more than two thousand homes had been completed.

Punta Gorda had a population of about eighteen thousand, with the larger city, Port Charlotte, just across twin bridges. As far as we were concerned the overall size of the immediate area was just fine with us.

With a county-wide population of just over one hundred thousand, we had most all of the services and shopping we needed without the construction and traffic of the more residential and commercially developed areas to the north and south of us.

As it turned out, it would be a few years before our little area of the Isles, known as the bird section, would begin to look residential.

This, of course, had its benefits, as Sabrina was able to meet and greet each newcomer on our daily walks.

Over the years I would joke that everyone knew her by name. When it came to Sabrina's parents, we were just along for the walk, known more often than not by a nod or just "Good morning."

At times I would joke with people that our child's attitude was, "*Everybody loves me. I think I'll run for mayor!*"

I think if our little girl had wanted to run for mayor, she might have had a shot at becoming the first canine to hold public office.

Over time, there weren't many people in the immediate area that didn't know her, and I can proudly state that their first impression of her was always the same, "Isn't she beautiful?" How did she respond to praise? She ate it up!

One of the few residents in the "hood," as it came to be known by our neighbors, had a sheltie named Laddie. He and Sabrina became fast friends. They used to communicate across the canal by barking back and forth when they were out on their respective lanais.

There's something to be said for empty spaces. Granted, you may not have many neighbors at first, but we sure did have peace and quiet.

I'll never forget one day in particular. The lot next door to us had a for sale sign on it from the time we'd arrived.

On this particular day, Sabina announced the arrival of humans as a car pulled up next door. Two people got out and started walking around, surveying the lot and looking more and more like potential buyers.

I got on the phone to Barb and Bill and suggested, sort of jokingly, that they send Laddie out onto the lanai, and we would do the same with Sabrina. The two dogs would start talking to each other and the noise would deter the lookers from getting serious about the property.

Well, so much for the best laid plans. Laddie and Sabrina did an admirable job. However, the people kept walking around and looking. No amount of noise seemed to chase them away.

Finally, I decided to go out and say hello. As it turned out, they weren't looking in the strictest sense, they were simply checking up on the lot that they'd owned for several years.

As we came to find out, they were live-aboard cruisers and had just returned from the Bahamas. Their sailboat was being worked on at a yard in Miami. So with time on their hands, they decided to rent a car and drive across to Punta Gorda to see what was happening in the Isles.

By now there were a half a dozen homes in the immediate area, and all of us knew each other.

We were about to hold the first neighborhood get-better-acquainted party at our house. So we invited the folks that owned the lot to come back and join us. After all, if they were going to build one day, they might as well begin to meet their neighbors.

They came to the party, and before we knew it they liked everyone so much they gave up the idea of one day building on the lot. Instead, Karen and Bob bought the house at the other end of our street that just happened to be for sale: lock, stock, and furniture and moved in.

As you might expect, they became best friends and ardent admirers of Sabrina.

I've often thought that God took extra time in creating dogs because somehow he managed to create a companion whose love knows no boundaries.

It's been said that our pets have the ability to change us, and living with Sabrina proved the point.

Over the years her outer calm tended to make me a more caring and thoughtful person. And as an aside, she definitely had a positive effect on my blood pressure, except of course when she was ill.

Although all of us say that we know and understand the word *love*, Sabrina had the remarkable ability to give the expression an entirely new meaning. She dispensed it morning, noon, and night, never asking for, or expecting it, to be returned.

No matter what you were doing or where you were in the house, you could always count on looking over your shoulder and seeing her either following behind or stretched out, chin on the floor, just watching and making sure that everything was as it should be.

At night her favorite spot was on the floor next to me as I sat in my glider rocker and either read or watched television.

Although she had an ample supply of toys, her idea of a good time was just being within arm's reach where she could be stroked or occasionally told what a good girl she was.

An alternate position that always seemed to amuse me was seeing her stretched out lengthwise in front of me, with her chin resting flat on the floor. Her eyes were wide open, and as she watched, she would occasionally sigh. The sigh, we determined, had to be one of contentment.

It took very little to please our girl. If she could speak I'm sure she would have told us, "*Just throw me a couple a carrots, and a Brussels sprout or two, and I'm yours.*"

One of the other "built-ins" Sabrina came equipped with was an alarm clock. She knew what time every treat was due and where she needed to be in order to receive it. If you failed to deliver at the appropriate time she would come to wherever you were and sit down in front of you with a big smile on her face!

If her smile failed to ring any bells, she would begin talking to you. If you still didn't get the message, those size fourteen paws of hers would begin whacking your legs. It was as if she was saying, "*Listen up, it's treat time. I don't ask for much, so pay attention. Get with the program and get me my treat!*"

Another alarm system that God installed in Sabrina was one of protection. When I took her out for the last time each night, the first thing she would do once on the grass was to stop and move in as close to my leg as possible. Her ears and tail would go down as she scanned the neighborhood. Believe it or not, she knew where every house, vehicle and person belonged. Sensing any danger or change in her surroundings, I could expect to hear the beginnings of a low rumble, leading to a full-throated growl. Once in full-protective mode, she wouldn't move a muscle until I reassured her that everything and everyone was where they belonged.

With her home life no longer in doubt and her meds keeping her stomach under control, Carla and I decided to take a chance and try taking a cruise vacation.

We visited several boarding kennels and finally selected a new one that was part of an equally new vet clinic.

The suites for large dogs, like the runs, were roomy, spotlessly clean, and long.

The people manning the boarding center seemed to really care about their guests, and unlike some of the facilities we visited, the building was air-conditioned.

So with more than a bit of concern about her stomach problems and the need for meds on a daily basis, we boarded our little girl, and left on a Mediterranean cruise.

The cruise was great: good food, nice people, and great historical stops. However, I found myself reaching for the telephone at each port in order to check up on her. With every call I was told she was doing just fine and not to worry. That was fine for them to say, but it did little to ease my concern.

Over the years, Carla made it abundantly clear that I was responsible for Sabrina's anxiety attacks. She said that I was the one that spoiled her, that I took her everywhere with me. She was right. I always wanted her with me and never stopped worrying about her when we were separated. No matter how I tried she was my biggest little girl!

Once we were in the car heading home from the port the good news we had received while traveling suddenly changed. I was told that after a few days in the boarding kennel her stomach became messed up, and she had to be put on a combination of anxiety reducing and stomach settling meds. We drove home, dropped our bags and went to get her — unpacking could wait!

When they brought her out, we were greeted with much crying and tail wagging, but did my little girl ever make me pay for our leaving her behind. It was clear to me that she didn't like my being gone because for the next forty-eight hours I got what could best be described as the canine cold shoulder. All I saw was her backside.

If you're a pet owner think back. How many times have you left your pet at home and upon returning garnered a response that surely meant, "*Go away, and leave me alone, will you? I'll show you!*"

A few years later, on our second and what turned out to be the last cruise we would take for several years, we decided to try a different tactic.

We figured that maybe if Sabrina was at home while we were gone rather than being boarded, she would handle her separation anxiety better.

One of the gals that worked for our vet agreed to come over to our house first thing in the morning, at lunchtime, and again in the evening. She would spend time talking to Sabrina, take her for walks, see to it that she had all of her meds and ample food and water.

This arrangement worked just fine for a couple of days. Then, on a noon visit she found Sabrina on the floor surrounded by meds and vitamin pills. My child had apparently gotten lonely, and being a very long dog, managed to stand up at the kitchen counter and using that long nose of hers took the daily dosage dispenser that held ten days of pills down to the floor where she managed to open it.

Our pet sitter gathered up and counted all the pills and miraculously, the only ones Sabrina had eaten were her vitamins. What a relief.

Refusing to chance leaving her home alone, she brought Sabrina back to Dr. Bivens office where she explained what had happened and her fear of leaving her on her own.

Normally, this would have been fine except for the fact our vet didn't have boarding kennels, just over-night cages for patients coming out of surgery.

However, not wanting to chance a repeat performance with the pills, and unbeknown to us, Dr. Bivens decided it would be better to put Sabrina into one of her largest overnight surgical cages and board her until we got back.

Those of you with pets know that most have a resident dog or cat that greets people as they come in for appointments. Well, Sabrina became the official greeter.

During the day she would stretch out behind the counter and wait for people to arrive. The moment they were in the lobby, she would stretch herself until her front paws were on the counter and, with a smile on her face and her tail wagging, make sure that everyone was greeted appropriately.

I have no doubt that if our child could talk she would have invited everyone to "*Come right in. Sit. Stay. Pay attention. Listen for your name to be called.*"

The actions of our vet ensured the fact that we would be lifelong customers. Of course, we did have to promise not to leave Sabrina at home again, as her becoming a boarder did manage to disrupt more than a few schedules.

As usual, I learned about our child's activities during one of my calls home. I'd discovered long distance overseas calling cards on the trip we were on thanks to one of the stewards on our ship, so I was armed and dangerous where telephones were concerned.

When we arrived home and went to pick Sabrina up, we found her manning her post at the front desk, and although we got a first class welcome, once again, upon arriving home, my child provided me with her backside. This time, the cold shoulder only lasted twenty-four hours.

I guess she wasn't quite as mad at me this time.

After experiencing difficulties while we were away on two cruises, we didn't need a building to fall on our heads in order to conclude that if we wanted to take a vacation in the future our child would be joining us.

Ah, the sacrifices you make for your children!

That was fine with me, because when we were apart I was as anxious as she was, worrying whether or not she'd be all right. I know this sounds corny, but that's the way it was. I'd count the days, and as we got close to home, I found myself counting the hours. Each night that we were apart I would communicate mentally, telling her to sleep well and to have good doggie dreams.

And some people say they're just pets!

Sabrina loved riding in the car. Under normal circumstances, the longer the ride, the better. For years I had driven sports cars. Sadly, Sabrina put an end to any potential mid or in my case, later-life crisis I might experience where cars were concerned. Suddenly, my car of choice had become a four-door sedan in order to provide my child with adequate head room. How mundane. I was beginning to look more and more like a Florida retiree.

"She's only a dog," you say. Well, how would I like being relegated to the back seat of a low-slung sports car? Talk about displeasure. Your ears always squished by the ceiling — your head bouncing off it every time the car went over a large bump in the road? I suspect your response would probably match Sabrina's, "*So, you had to have a sports car! How would you like to ride around with your ears folded down because the roof is too low? Well, how would you like it!*

Well, if sacrifice on my part ensured that my little girl was comfortable, I was happy to oblige. Her comfort was my responsibility to deliver. The backseat of my car belonged to her.

Over the years she never once tried to get in the front seat. It was as if she knew the back seat was hers.

Once in the car she would sit at attention behind me and review the neighborhood as it passed us by. If she saw another dog, she would immediately remind them that this was her neighborhood and that she would be back!

Having left the area, she would stretch out and enjoy the ride. However, by some mysterious navigational quirk, she instinctively knew when we had re-entered the neighborhood and I could expect to look in the rear view mirror and see her sitting up, at attention.

Over time Carla said that the two of us must be joined at the hip. If I was gone for more than a few minutes, Sabrina greeted my return with cries of joy, a lot of shaking, tail wagging, and licks. When Carla and I were away on a trip, I found myself missing Sabrina the moment our trip began and counting the hours until we returned home — worrying whether my child was alright.

Carla often said that if a stranger was watching Sabrina when I arrived home they would have thought I'd abandoned our child and then changed my mind. Abandonment, of course, was never an option.

My sister and brother-in-law and their kids, as well as my parents, lived on the east coast of Florida. My sister lived in Palm Beach Gardens, with my parents a few miles to the south of them.

I'd looked for a home on the East Coast for a while but trips to visit family convinced me that it was far too crowded.

And where waterfront property was concerned, it was too pricey for our retirement planning.

Once we moved to Punta Gorda, hardly a month went by when we weren't making the hundred-and-fifty-mile drive to the east coast for a visit.

Large dogs weren't allowed in the small retirement community where my parents lived. However, we did manage to smuggle Sabrina in and out for short visits.

My sister's small dog didn't much care for large dogs and Sabrina felt the same way about small ones so when we were planning to stay overnight we found a motel that allowed pets. This enabled us to lengthen our visits.

As long as she was with us, Sabrina was a good traveler. She could be crated for several hours as long as we left the TV on so she could watch the cartoon channel. For some reason this seemed to capture her attention and keep her occupied.

One of the interesting asides to Sabrina was the fact that she seemed to instinctively know when not to let her size and weight overpower anyone.

My mom and dad first met Sabrina while we were in Tennessee. Over the years my father always liked dogs; however, the same couldn't be said of my mother. She tolerated them for very short periods of time.

Once we'd moved to Florida and were visiting family on a regular basis, we assumed that my mother would become a real challenge for Sabrina.

Not so. She made it a point to re-introduce herself to my parents immediately. Failing to take a brush off from my mother as anything but an opportunity requiring extra effort on her part, Sabrina went to work!

Before long she had both my parents wrapped around and eating out of her paws.

Mom and Dad were already in their mid-eighties and becoming frail when Sabrina entered their lives on a regular basis. Somehow she seemed to know that when walking with one or both of them she had to move with great care. At no time did she ever cause them to lose their balance or fall. Quite the opposite, she was a four-legged security blanket.

She would walk alongside them outdoors, moving at their speed and checking periodically to make sure they were looking down at her from time to time.

Because she'd been through several training classes, including obedience training, my father proudly introduced her to friends and neighbors as his "four-legged grandchild with a PhD, Doctor of Dogs, degree."

As years passed and my parents moved into an assisted living facility, Sabrina, once again, was one of the few dogs allowed to visit.

I'll never forget the time she had everyone on the building nursing staff on their toes.

Because my parents were gradually becoming frail, the assisted living people attached a tennis ball to a string that connected to their "call for aid" button between their chairs in the den, thinking they'd find it easier to grasp a ball than a ring if they needed assistance.

Sabrina, seeing the ball, must have decided, "*Gee, what a neat orange ball. I think I'll bat it around and play with it.*"

Well, it didn't take long for my girl to discover that that tennis ball wasn't a toy, and you can probably guess the rest. She rang the hell out of that bell until the assisted living nurses finally arrived and found the evidence in her mouth.

Everyone kind of laughed and thought it funny, but in retrospect, it really wasn't funny. It had taken my parents' assisted living caregivers far too long to respond, and it left us wondering what would have happened had there been a real emergency.

It also made me wonder if Sabrina was trying to tell me something about her beloved Grampy and Grammy. Maybe they weren't being taken care of as well as they should have been. Meetings with their caregivers brought promises of quicker response.

Most of the elderly folks in my parents' building loved Sabrina. She returned the favor in kind, whether riding up on the elevator or just greeting everyone as she walked across the lobby.

When someone tried to initiate a ban on large dogs being allowed inside the building, Sabrina was afforded a special entrance. To the best of our knowledge, she was the only dog of size that we had ever seen in the building.

With the approval of the general manager of the facility, we were allowed to sneak her up the back stairs. He knew how much it meant to my parents to have her visit and, having watched her with elderly people, knew she wasn't a threat to anyone.

When my mother was sent to a rehab facility, the result of a physical setback, Sabrina was, once again, allowed to visit.

Clowns come in all sizes and shapes. Big and small, fat and thin. Sabrina may not have had a red ball on the end of her nose or floppy shoes on her rather large feet, but she had the ability to make everyone around her smile!

On one of her visits to the rehab facility, we were told that my mother was down the hall in the television room.

When we got there, there were several elderly folks in one stage of recuperation or another sitting in a circle watching television.

Sabrina nuzzled all of them and laid down where she could keep a watchful on her newfound friends.

A nurse came into the room and walked to a small side room where she filled a water pitcher with ice cubes from an icemaker.

To Sabrina that was a call to attention, thinking I'm sure, *I know that sound.*

That was all my child had to hear. It was show time!

No one liked ice cubes more than my little girl. At home she would head for the refrigerator the minute she heard the icemaker delivering cubes.

Like most everything else in the house, she thought the icemaker was created and installed exclusively for her enjoyment.

When we were preparing to sit down for a meal she would sit in front of the refrigerator waiting an opportunity to crunch and enjoy one or two "cubers" as we called them, as we filled our water glasses.

When we had company for dinner she would sit in the next room, waiting for our guests to throw cubes to her one at a time. She would catch every one of them, then smile, crunch, and wait for the enthusiastic response of her audience.

This day was no different. I got a couple of cubes from the machine and tossed them to her. She caught and crunched them and when finished looked longingly for more.

Her audience all but applauded. People were smiling from ear to ear, and before long everyone in the room was pitching her ice cubes. She was in ice cube heaven and enjoying every minute of it. Give my little girl an opportunity to ham it up, and she is W.C. Fields with four legs and a tail.

Aside from being the most even-tempered child I have ever known, she was also the biggest showoff on four legs.

Sabrina made several trips with us back to Tennessee to visit Carla's family during the holidays.

It didn't matter whether she was traveling five miles or half way across country, once properly medicated, as long as she was with us her stomach problem remained under control.

That didn't mean that the delicate balance needed to keep her on an even keel didn't rear its ugly head from time to time. In one rather unusual instance, we almost lost her.

We'd sold our first sailboat after fourteen years, feeling it was too small for a dog of Sabrina's size. Hoping to make a cruiser out of her, we purchased a larger boat.

Carla and I had taken the new boat out for a training lesson, leaving Sabrina home in our master bath. We had placed baby gates across the doorway, thinking it would deter her from trying to escape into the house. That proved to be a near fatal mistake. The jaws of a German shepherd are among the strongest of the breeds, and when she set hers to removing those baby gates, they came apart as if they were made of matchsticks.

Sabrina hated to be alone, so in her mind I'm sure she concluded, "*I don't see any guards. I'll just get rid of this gate and go find my parents.*"

Having made good her escape into the bedroom, and finding that we weren't in the house, she did just that. She set out to find us.

We'd left a very large and heavy bedroom window open a few inches. As best we could tell, once she returned to the bedroom and knowing she had to get outside to conduct her search, somehow she managed to get her nose and then her entire body between the windowsill and the open window. Using sheer strength and determination, she managed to lift the entire window.

Next, she proceeded to break out the screen covering the window and escaped on to the enclosed pool deck.

Here's where God must have been smiling upon us.

Fortunately, our neighbors across the canal, Steve and Cindi Murphy, were out on their lanai. One minute they saw Sabrina on the pool deck, the next, she was gone.

Knowing that she was never allowed outside alone and that a pool cover hid the pool from sight, Steve and Cindi, fearing the worst, reacted. They ran around the canal sea wall and broke into our pool cage in time to haul Sabrina out from under the pool solar cover.

Had they not seen her and acted quickly, our little girl, being bound and determined to find us, probably would have drowned. Chances are she wouldn't have known how to get out from under the pool cover, much less how to find her way up the steps and out of the pool.

When we returned from a day of sailing, we found several of our neighbors standing on the dock with a very wet German shepherd. Steve and Cindi were only too happy to tell us what Madame Houdini had attempted.

I guess you could say that nothing was going to stop our little girl when she set her mind to finding us.

As we listened to our neighbors and later surveyed Sabrina's handiwork, I could just picture our child paddling around Charlotte Harbor, checking every boat until she found the right one.

Knowing her fierce determination, and given half a chance, that's probably what she would have done, assuming she found her way to the harbor.

As it turned out, even our new boat wasn't large enough to accommodate Sabrina. So much for any thoughts of cruising vacations with our child standing on deck barking orders.

Carla and I have always had a fascination with Civil War history and on several occasions planned, but never seemed to find the time, to do a Civil War battlefield tour by car.

This probably sounds strange when you consider the fact that we were retired, but, believe it or not, days just seemed to fly by.

Finally, after much procrastination and with Sabrina reviewing the roadmaps, the three of us set off on a two-week car tour that would take us from Florida to Gettysburg and down to Charleston.

Do our pets really care where we take them?

As we headed out on our great adventure, I wondered what Sabrina was thinking. Was she really happy to be spending long hours in the car with us, or was she thinking, "*Finally. The dog finally gets to go on a vacation, and where do we go — Disney World? Sea World? No such luck. Oh well, at least they didn't leave me behind this time!*"

Sabrina took the entire trip in stride. She listened intently to park tapes as we did battlefield driving tours, and walked several of the battlefields with us.

At Gettysburg, we hired a park guide for an entire day. You should have seen his face when he opened the car door, began to climb in, and realized what was sitting on the backseat waiting to greet him.

To say he was taken aback would be an understatement. However, once he got over the initial shock and was officially introduced to our little historian, he and Sabrina became fast friends.

Later, she and I shared the backseat as our guide drove us around several special areas of the Gettysburg battleground. And, no, I didn't share my sandwich with her during our lunch break.

As it turned out, Sabrina was allowed to walk most of the national parks with us, including several stops during our Gettysburg tour.

At Appomattox she waited patiently, first with me and then with Carla as we took turns touring the house where Grant and Lee wrote an end to the Civil War.

We'd started early this particular morning, and there were no tourists or buses at the site when we arrived. So after our tour of the house, she joined Carla and I as we listened to the park ranger share some of the little known facts about that important day in our country's history.

Never having made it to Cape Canaveral, and with the trip going extremely well, we threw in a couple days at the end of our battlefields tour and treated ourselves to a surprise stop at the Cape.

The Cape and Fort Sumter in Charleston harbor were the only times that Sabrina had to watch television in our motel room — dogs weren't allowed on those tours.

For over two weeks and several thousand miles, Sabrina was never a problem, and we were never refused lodging at a hotel or motel. In fact, at one stop, a new Holiday Inn Atrium, she was even invited to join us in the restaurant for dinner.

Whether we were checking in, or it was time to check out, Sabrina would stretch her long body to the fullest, put her front paws on the lobby counter, and with her ever present smile, say good morning or goodbye to whoever was working the front desk. Always the lady, if they came around front to meet her, she would either extend a paw to shake their hand or provide a couple of "licks."

Over the years Sabrina was my favorite listener. In fact, she was one of the few people who never responded negatively to anything I had to say. I could talk with her for hours, and she would sit in rapt attention, her head moving and tilting from one side to the other as she hung on my every word.

In her mind she was probably thinking, "*He loves it when I look like I'm paying attention. Frankly, I don't understand a thing he's saying.*"

If during the course of our conversation she decided it was time to go out and take care of business, she would come to attention, advise me of her need with a bark, and if I failed to pay attention, you guessed it, she would take those big paws of hers and whack me, then run to the door and sit.

She always seemed to know just what was needed in order to get what she wanted.

At times she seemed more human than a human.

Just as she had a fetish for ice cubes, she was also a popcorn junkie.

The minute Carla reached for a bag of popcorn to pop, she would begin dancing and prancing around the kitchen. She knew that there would be three bowls, one for each of us. Although where she was concerned, hers was butter and salt free.

When it came time for popcorn, she didn't just bury her nose in a bowl and devour it. Not on your life. She'd move back several feet from me, sit up straight, and demand that I throw her a kernel at a time.

I could throw her popcorn all night, and she rarely missed a kernel. I don't know whether she had great eye to mouth coordination or great depth perception. What I do know is that she enjoyed catching popped kernels so I indulged her. I used to pretend I was announcing a baseball game — calling out catches in the outfield as I threw to her.

She probably felt a little like Rodney Dangerfield. "*How stupid was that? Go ahead, make the dog show off for everything. I don't get no respect!*"

For Mother's Day and on Carla's birthday Sabrina always made sure to include a six-pack of popcorn along with a card for her favorite mother. We implied to friends that this gesture took the majority of her allowance. In reality, it was her way of insuring a continuing supply of popcorn.

As I've said several times, my child had a style and grace that was pure showoff, and I, along with most everyone else, enjoyed watching her!

Sabrina never made any daring rescues. Never saved any lives. She never made the headlines. Yet she left everyone she came in contact with smiling.

She would prance around with a look that said, "*Hey, I'm a German shepherd. If there was someone to rescue, I'll be first in line to volunteer!*"

If she knew that you weren't a dog lover, and a couple of our friends weren't, she would work doubly hard to win you over, and more often than not, she did just that!

She would sit in front of you and just look at you.

If that didn't get your attention and produce a pat on the head, she would talk to you.

If you were still holding out, she would bring you her toys, one at a time, and drop them in your lap.

In short, she would wear you down, never giving in until you smiled. She always prevailed. Failure was not an option as far as she was concerned.

She was a friend to everyone — well, almost everyone. For some reason she never liked the sight of the brown UPS truck.

Federal Express, Airborne, the mail man, all were welcome at her front door. When she saw the brown UPS truck coming down the street she made it perfectly clear that he was not welcome in her neighborhood. If the delivery was for us, the driver would hustle up to our screen door, drop the package, and beat a hasty retreat to the safety of his truck.

If he only knew that she was all bark and no bite!

Carla and I used to tell people that Sabrina's bark and growl would scare most intruders away from the house as long as they didn't see her. However, should anyone gain entry, she would probably show them around and ask if they wanted a light snack before departing.

That was my girl!

She was always nearby, whether sleeping on the floor next to me at night or just joining me on a short car trip or a walk in the "hood."

When it was my mother's time to pass, Sabrina was at her bedside, licking her hand. Somehow, it was as if she knew that she might never see her granny again and just wanted her to know that she was right there beside her.

That's love! I didn't fully understand it at the time, but thinking back on this moment, isn't that what unconditional love is all about — "giving, with no strings attached — no concern for what you will receive in return?"

If I was asked to describe my wife and our relationship, those are the words I would choose!

I'm a Gator Too

It wasn't a day like every other as Carla and I headed north on interstate seventy-five. We were on our way to Gainesville, home of the University of Florida. Sabrina was stretched out on the back seat fast asleep — not a care in the world.

No, we weren't about to send our big girl off to college.

Rather we had two hundred miles to think about what lay ahead for her when we arrived, and the thoughts weren't very pleasant.

Both my son and daughter graduated from the University of Florida and are rabid Gator fans. So when Sabrina found it necessary to travel to Gainesville, I'm sure she felt that this qualified her to become a full-fledged member of the Gator canine nation.

Unfortunately, her stay on campus this trip didn't allow time to pledge a sorority or schedule classes. It wasn't that kind of trip. This trip would involve a neurosurgeon and possible brain surgery.

Once Sabrina's stomach problem was diagnosed and brought under control, Carla and I looked ahead, with fingers crossed, to many years of good health and love for our girl.

The prednisone that was so much a part of her daily regimen had caused her weight to balloon to over one hundred pounds. Excess weight, well beyond the norm for a female, can be as damaging to pets as it is in humans. So you can imagine its effect on a dog, especially during our long, hot Florida summers.

Noting her continued weight gain during periodic checkups, Dr. Ward suggested we cut out all dog treats in an effort to bring her weight down.

Bummer! Imagine being told you could no longer have dehydrated carrots and sweet potatoes when you'd never met one you didn't like.

As usual Sabrina took her latest diet restrictions in stride and turned "a glass half empty" into one that was full to overflowing.

"Glass overflowing — my paw! It's easy for you to say. I'm the one giving up the goodies again!"

New vegetables were substituted and every now and again I'd sneak my girl a canine treat.

In the past, Carla would buy several pounds of carrots and sweet potatoes at a time and dehydrate them down to small chews. You'd be shocked to see what was left of ten pounds of carrots once the water is extracted from them. I know I was. Well, those days were over — at least until Sabrina lost thirty pounds.

We continued to keep bite size raw carrots in the refrigerator. They were used as is, but only as an extra special treat, as they contained considerable sugar.

Brussels sprouts and other vegetables from Carla's garden became Sabrina's new taste treats. She liked the Brussels sprouts so much that we were able to hide her pills in them and toss them to her one at a time. This combination of catch and swallow worked like a charm and it eliminated the task of having to open her mouth and place a pill as far in as possible — then quickly hold her muzzle closed until she swallowed. Not exactly fun! Do you remember how you responded to veggies as a kid? Not so with our big girl. Place a pill along with a vegetable in your hand, and she would sit up straight, open her mouth wide, and anxiously await their insertion.

"Hide, schmide. They're not fooling anyone. They're just lucky I like my veggies!"

And, did she ever. Also on her list of favorites were: cauliflower, broccoli, green beans, peas and peppers. Say the word, and Sabrina world run to the kitchen and wait anxiously for one of her new treats.

Once you've known fear, where a loved one is concerned, it is difficult to erase it from your memory. In Sabrina's case, that feeling was about to begin rearing its ugly head, over and over again — I just didn't know it!

Sabrina and I had been out for a walk. It was a beautiful day and we were enjoying the walk when suddenly, just short of our house, she stopped, looked up at me, and collapsed.

I can guess what you're thinking, and no, she didn't simply stop and lay down. She went down!

Now I'm a pretty big guy, but unfortunately, after several spinal operations and an on-going fight with a narrowing spinal canal, lifting and carrying her home was out of the question. Much as I wanted to, that wasn't in the cards.

As she lay on the road looking up at me, my heart sank. I got down on the ground and began stroking her head and talking to her.

She raised her head, rested it in my free hand and just looked at me. Her eyes were moving around like the pictures on a one-armed bandit. When her eyes stopped moving they seemed to roll back into her head. At that moment I felt helpless!

Those beautiful brown eyes of hers seemed to be everywhere at once. I couldn't leave her in the street.

It took all the strength I could muster to concentrate on the problem at hand. Rather than just sit there, hold her, and cry, I did the one thing I felt would get the two of us closer to the house.

There is nothing more heart breaking than watching a small child that's in pain yet is too young to communicate. Believe me when I tell you that the same holds true when the situation involves our pets.

If you're wondering if I'm equating Sabrina to a child, you're right, I am. I know dog experts say, "They're just animals, treat them as such," but as far as I'm concerned, that's a crock!

One thing you may have heard about German shepherds is the fact that they are extremely loyal and strong-willed. In fact, they will do almost anything, no matter the pain, in an effort to please their owner or pack leader.

This was a moment when the bond Sabrina and I shared really stepped front and center.

We were only a couple hundred feet from the house when she went down. Everything that happened that afternoon probably only took a minute or two, but to me it felt as if time stood still. All I could think at the time was, *I'm not going to lose her. I'm not going to leave her here in the street. We will get home!*

Looking at her, I could feel her telling me, "*Please, Dad, don't leave me here.*"

There was no way I was going to leave her and go for help. I had no idea what she would do if she saw me running away.

So I did the first thing that came to mind — I stood up and commanded her to heel. At first she didn't respond. Then, miraculously, she stood on four very wobbly legs and together we began to move ahead a few steps at a time.

My big girl went down several times on the way to our front door, but each time I spoke, she responded, willing herself to stand up and move forward.

I know what the hot shot trainers say, "Don't get too emotional, they're pets. Establish boundaries and limitations, and treat them as pets."

Don't kid yourself. I've never met a cat or dog lover that didn't break into a smile when he or she talked about his or her four-legged "child."

I knew I was responsible for a good deal of Sabrina's separation anxiety. Carla never stopped reminding me!

Yes, I taught her the boundaries and limitations that were expected of her, and she respected them. After that, I spoiled the hell out of her.

Guilty as charged!

If love existed between the two of us, it was never more visible than during the few hundred feet we covered together that day.

I don't think I was ever more proud of her than I was that afternoon as I willed her to get up, telling her over and over that I knew she could do it. She went down time and again, but she never stopped moving forward.

Once we were near the front door I had her lie down and to "stay." I went the last few feet, opened the door and called out to Carla. When she came out, I quickly explained what had happened.

We didn't bother to call our vet; Carla just backed a car out of the garage. Using a large bath towel we fashioned a sling. Between the two of us, and with a little help from Sabrina, we managed to get her into the car.

Dr. Bivens saw her immediately. Sabrina's eyes were still moving around, but as it turned out, her heart was strong and her pulse was slowly beginning to return to normal. Once the examination was complete we still had no clear-cut idea what caused her to suddenly collapse.

Dr. Bivens felt the problem was brain induced. Knowing this was beyond her capabilities, she suggested referring us on to the University of Florida, Veterinary School of Medicine, in Gainesville. We agreed.

She made the call and, indicating that this might well be an emergency, was able to set up an appointment for the next day.

So, here we were, heading into the unknown one more time. I was driving while at the same time trying not to think about the potential consequences of the trip — it wasn't easy. Every time I allowed my mind to wander the tears would start. Next thing I knew, Carla and I were switching off driving, as neither one of us could concentrate on the road for very long.

While we sat up front worrying, Sabrina was sleeping like a baby in back — oblivious to her parent's anguish. We had no idea what we'd find when we arrived at the Veterinary Medical Center. Let me tell you, it turned out to be quite an eye opener.

As we waited to see the doctor we'd spoken with on the phone, we had a chance to speak with several pet owners. Concern is a shared experience!

Some of the dogs in the waiting area were in various stages of surgical after-care. Others, like Sabrina, had been referred to the University Veterinary Medical Center by their vet back home. In many cases it was a court of last resort.

Hardly anyone was from the immediate area. Like us many had driven hundreds of miles in search of a solution to their pet's problem. They'd come from Alabama, Georgia, South Carolina, and of course, Florida. That in and of itself made a statement about the quality of care and expertise one could expect.

We watched as doctors, residents, interns, and students came out to meet their patients. The caring that was exhibited was beyond anything we might have expected. Maybe it was because in many instances these beloved animals and their owners were reaching out for a last chance insofar as a solution to their pets' medical needs, were concerned.

I've always said, "no matter how bad you feel, go to a hospital and look around, you can always find someone in worse condition." I'm here to tell you that this can be said of pets as well!

Finally, Sabrina was called, and we met with her doctor for a few minutes. Dr. Heidi Barnes was the chief resident in the neurology department. We liked her immediately.

Sabrina greeted her with the usual smile and tail wags, and after some discussion we watched as the two of them went off together — just two old pals going for a walk.

Of course, this took place after Sabrina did her customary "find me if you can" trick, hiding under two chairs.

Like us, Sabrina was a Star Trek junkie. When it came to doctors, the moment she was in their office she would go into hiding under my chair.

Now when you're as big as my girl, hiding doesn't come easy, but we concluded that if she thought she was a Klingon with a cloak of invisibility, so be it.

Once under my chair, hiding behind my legs, she'd fire up her invisibility shield and disappear. Actually, her cloak didn't work all that well because no matter how she tried, either her head or her butt and tail could be seen sticking out.

Doctors all said this was the puppy in her, and they were right. The years may have been adding up, but my baby was just that — a big, loveable, and sweet puppy in adult clothing.

To look at her at that moment, you never would have known anything was wrong with her. Her outlook on life never changed, but sadly, once again, her health was about to do just that!

We'd been waiting for what seemed an eternity but was probably little over an hour, when an intern came forward and called our name. She ushered us into a small room and, after a brief discussion, advised us that Sabrina and Dr. Barnes would be with us momentarily.

If you think you can will someone you love out of your mind when times are tough — you can't!

When they appeared, Dr. Barnes explained her belief that Sabrina's problem was related to her skull and advised us that she wanted to perform a brain and CAT scan in order to pin down or allay her suspicions.

She indicated that if she was right, they would like to keep Sabrina overnight and perform whatever surgery was required the next day.

At the time, I had no idea that such tests existed for pets, and when I heard what she wanted to do and the potential need for surgery, my concern went from fear to tears!

The day was rapidly turning into my worst nightmare as we told Dr. Barnes to move ahead and do whatever was necessary.

She told us that Sabrina would be put to sleep and that the tests and recovery would take several hours. As we were approaching the noon hour she suggested we might want to go out and get something to eat, then come back and wait for the results.

Neither of us felt much like eating, but we went anyway. At least it would kill time.

As it appeared we probably wouldn't learn anything until late in the day, and we couldn't be sure what was ahead, we decided to check in to one of the motels the medical center indicated was pet friendly.

With many of their patients coming from outside the state, I'm sure the university drummed up a lot of business for the local hotels and motels — except during football season. You don't want to be looking for a room in Gainesville during a Gator football weekend.

When we returned from lunch we continued to compare notes with folks waiting for word on their pets. Some were back for a second and third time, and the stories and prior medical results they had experienced were amazing. Some of the solutions, though bordering on a miracle, were also heart breaking.

Somehow you don't think in terms of cancer, heart problems, amputations, or transplants for pets, but there they seemed to be an everyday occurrence. We found more than a few individuals in the same frame of mind as we were. All of us were going through one level of mental anguish and concern or another and handling it as best we could.

Carla had given me a plaque for Christmas one year that read, "German shepherds leave their paw prints on your heart."

How true. Sabrina hadn't just left paw prints on my heart, she'd walked all over it, and then she stole it.

They say there's safety in numbers, and there could be something to that. As we sat and waited for the results of the tests, it was comforting to know that we weren't alone — the lobby was filled with parents either with or waiting for their loved ones!

Unbeknown to us, in a matter of hours we would be faced with a new bridge to cross, and my big girl would have to live with another medical obstacle for the rest of her life.

If a young child couldn't understand what was happening at a time like this, what could you expect as your pet looked into your eyes, trusting your every sound, yet never understanding a word you were saying? Telling Sabrina not to worry, that everything was going to be just fine, seemed useless at the time, but we knew it was the best we could do until she was returned to us.

Late in the afternoon Dr. Barnes returned with Sabrina in tow and advised us that she had bi-lateral vestibular disease, and that, yes, she would like permission to operate the next day.

She explained that the infection lay behind both ears and that both eardrums would need to be punctured as part of the surgery. She said she was confident Sabrina would do just fine. Of course, because they would be working in delicate areas, her positive attitude came with all of the usual surgical warnings — warnings guaranteed to scare the hell out of you.

She advised us that the surgery would provide relief from what had become a deep inner ear problem. She also pointed out that she could not guarantee that the problem would not resurface, but that with regular care we could expect to control the problem.

We were told that in the future we'd have to pay close attention to her ears. They would need to be checked and cleaned out with a liquid solution on a regular basis for the rest of her life.

As it turned out, the one bit of good news was the fact that if we wanted to take Sabrina with us that night, Dr. Barnes said she would release her to us. However, she explained that we would have to have her back at the clinic early the next morning as they would not be posting the surgical schedules until then, and she had no idea where Sabrina's scheduled surgery time would fall.

Surprisingly, she also gave us all of her phone and beeper numbers, including her home phone number and told us to feel free to call if we had questions or concerns once we were back at the motel.

We were only too happy to take our girl back to the motel with us. The idea of leaving her alone at the hospital overnight would have probably been more difficult for us than it would have been for her. I guess Dr. Barnes could tell by the way we were reacting to the news that we needed each other that night.

I am not a control freak, but as president and chief operating officer of a group of companies before I retired, I knew the importance of staying focused and asking questions.

Over time, you find that you enjoy a second sense when things aren't going right, and you move to correct the situation or, at least, better understand it before allowing things to get out of hand.

Not in this instance. I felt as though I was running — out of control. I couldn't adjust or make changes. I didn't even know the right questions to ask. All I could do was listen, hold on to my big girl, and pray.

Much as I hate to admit it, once we were back at the motel for the night, and I was on the floor petting and talking to Sabrina, I felt totally inept — useless. Nothing I could say or do seemed to minimize the pain I was feeling — and she was the one that was looking at delicate surgery in the morning, not me!!

I promised that Dr. Barnes was going to make her better, knowing all along that she didn't have a clue what was going to happen to her in the morning.

Our pets may not understand what we are saying, but I believe there's a link between us, often described as a bond. There's a look our pet children give us when something is wrong. It's as if they're reaching deep inside us for a show of faith and understanding.

That's the way it was with Sabrina and I.

Dr. Barnes must have known what we were going through because she called us after making her rounds that night to once again tell us not to worry, that she'd take good care of Sabrina.

Maybe she made the same call to all of her patient's owners, we'll never know. However, at that moment she became much more than just a doctor. This wasn't just another surgery. She really cared!

Before trying to call it a night I spoke to God.

I took a prescription sleeping pill that night hoping it would turn off my mind and knock me out. It didn't! As it turned out, I hardly slept at all.

Someone once told me that during times of stress if you take long slow breaths and count slowly backward from one hundred you will fall asleep.

I counted and then counted again. It didn't work!

I spent a good part of the night asking God why this was happening and asking for his help. Not for me, but for my little girl. At times I wondered if he thought the two of us were one where my requests were concerned.

We had Sabrina at the clinic by seven the next morning and shortly thereafter an intern came down to take her up to the surgical floor. We hugged her, and as she looked back over her shoulder I told her once again that everything was going to be just fine.

It might have been a lie, who's to say? But you can never, ever stop thinking positively where your loved ones are concerned. Somehow I wanted her to believe that she was just going for a walk and would come back to us soon.

For the next several hours I found myself looking at my watch and then the clock on the wall.

Then I reversed course and began looking at the clock on the wall before checking my watch.

Sabrina's life seemed to be spinning out of control. We had done all that we could. Now, it was time to pray once again and continue counting minutes.

Whenever I stopped clock watching, I started thinking, and when I started thinking, the tears started flowing. I found myself rushing out into the parking lot to be alone.

Finally, we were advised that it would be early afternoon before there would be any news, so the clock watching and pacing continued.

This beautiful, four-legged creature that had been with us for what seemed far too little time was in God's and Dr. Heidi Barnes's skilled hands.

The phrase "time is such a fleeting thing" obviously wasn't coined by someone waiting for word from a surgeon. The minutes dragged into hours as the morning seemed to limp into afternoon.

An intern came down to tell us that Sabrina was out of surgery and that Dr. Barnes would be with us once she finished her other surgical obligations.

Late in the afternoon she finally came down, and we could tell by the smile on her face that everything must have gone well.

It had, but what she told us scared the hell out of me. As she expected, both of her eardrums had to be pierced in order to reach an infection that was lodged deep behind each ear. She said she'd been able to get at all of the infection. Sabrina was out of recovery and resting quietly in a recovery cage. If we wanted to stick around, she could be released to us in a few hours after one more checkup.

Dr. Barnes reviewed the medications Sabrina would be on and the care that needed to be taken when checking and washing out her ears. She explained that we would need to do this on a regular basis for the rest of her life!

She told us that she'd like to see Sabrina a couple of times over the next few months and suggested we plan appointments in three and then eight weeks.

Medications and the solution to be used in her ears would be given to us when we checked out. Our vet would be able to write future refill prescriptions.

We were thrilled and amazed by the news that Sabrina would be able to leave the hospital in a few hours. How do they do it? Our pets seem to bounce back from surgery far faster than we humans.

We advised Dr. Barnes that due to the late hour we would be staying in Gainesville over night. She thought that was a good idea just in case there were any complications during the night.

So once again we waited. A couple of hours later we could see our child coming down the hall with Dr. Barnes hanging on to her leash. Sabrina's tail was wagging and that ever-present smile was front and center. To look at the way she was carrying on it was hard to believe she had just come through major surgery. She was acting as if nothing had happened.

I have no idea whether she was in pain, but the minute she saw us her tail went in to overdrive, and the cries of joy began. I don't know who was happier, her or us. As always it was a toss-up.

Dr. Barnes told us to call her that night if we had any questions, and as with the night before, she didn't wait for us to call, she called us to check on her patient. It appeared that Sabrina had made another friend.

The next morning we had breakfast, said the magic word *car*, and before you could say presto-change-o the big girl was bounding into her seat, positioned, and ready to give directions. So much for college!

I'm sure she was thinking, "*Let's get out of here. I've had all the education I can stand, thank you very much!*"

Needless to say, the ride home was much better than the ride up. We knew we had work to do where her health was concerned, but once again, our child was on the road to recovery.

We'd heard numerous stories about the longevity of German shepherds and all fell short of my demand that Sabrina wait until I died before she was called back home.

Hip dysphasia was another major concern of ours. It was a chronic problem that led to the early departure of far too many shepherds and other large dogs, but knock on wood, X-rays of our girl showed no sign of this.

Although she escaped this problem, a few years later we would learn that she had torn a cruciate ligament in one of her hind legs while chasing a ball, but this didn't sound life threatening.

Again and again I found myself thanking God for loaning Sabrina to us — repeating over and over my vow that no matter what it took, I would always be there for her. I had promised she would never live in pain needlessly, and I intended to keep that promise.

If Sabrina was listening as I communicated with God, she probably would have told me, "*And don't think I won't remind you if you ever forget!*"

Deep down, I think God knew that he could count on me to honor my promise no matter how difficult it might be to keep — including when he asked that she be returned!

It was at this point in my time with Sabrina that I began to wonder if I picked her, she picked me, or if God was responsible for bringing the two of us together?

I wonder how many pet owners have asked the same question. We travel through life making acquaintances. Yet, how many people do we know that we can actually call a "friend"— someone that is there for us no matter what — that is willing to give of himself freely, and without reservation?

Love Doesn't Come with a Price Tag

Sabrina had been living with medical problems from the day she was born; we just didn't know it in those early puppy months.

She'd already been through one major surgery and would remain on a variety of meds for life, but you never would have known it to look at her — she was a puppy for life.

Every day provided her with a new opportunity to spread laughter, love, and affection. She did this with a smile painted on her face from the time she woke up until the time I kissed her good night, told her to have good doggy dreams and to dream of angels.

You've already heard me say that Sabrina had a remarkably high tolerance for pain. No matter what was happening to her, she simply accepted the fact that this was the way things were meant to be and went on about her activities without a care in the world. However, before long this would change in ways Carla or I could not begin to imagine.

We had been out for a day of sailing.

Sabrina was safely tucked away in her crate with no chance of escape.

The return trip from the harbor through the canals to our home takes about forty-five minutes. It's a "no wake" zone from the moment you enter the canal system.

It had been a beautiful day. The sails were covered, and we were motoring along, enjoying what breeze we could find. We were talking about nothing in particular when one of our neighbors, Paula and Steve Johnson, pulled up behind us in their boat.

Paula had a new camera and was shooting everything in sight. Over the radio she asked permission to come alongside and take some pictures of our boat, so we slowed, and she shot away.

The next day she and Steve dropped by for a visit and to give us the pictures she'd taken. Sabrina treated every visitor as an equal opportunity to show off. She immediately found her newest ball and came prancing into the living room where we were sitting to show it to Steve.

Sabrina never offered you a toy — at first. She would lean forward and allow you to take a good look at her prize, then pull her head back and dance away. No growling or tug of war, she just wanted to show you what was new.

Well, this day she decided to return to Steve several times with her ball. Knowing she wouldn't give it to him, Steve pretended to ignore her. So the big girl decided to drop it in his lap in order to get his undivided attention.

I guess in this instance her thinking was," *If you won't try and take it, I'll just give it to you.*"

Steve picked up the ball and tossed it a few feet from the living room into the dining room. Sabrina took off on the tile floor to retrieve it. As she came to a stop her hind legs went out from under her on the smooth tile floor, and she belly flopped and skidded her way to the ball.

None of us thought anything of her landing at the time. We threw the balls and other toys to her several times a day and flying flops were frequently used to retrieve them.

It wasn't until several days later that we noticed that when she walked, her right hind leg seemed to be coming down at an angle that just didn't look right.

We called Dr. Bivens and made an appointment to bring her in to be checked.

At first nothing seemed to be wrong with her. Just like we humans, somehow she managed to mask or will the problem to go away when she got to the doctor. Believe it or not, her leg showed no signs of damage; she was walking just fine. So we went home.

We didn't stop throwing balls, and she didn't stop careening across our tile floors to get them.

Deep down, I really think the tear that would be found a couple months later just didn't show up on X-rays on our first visit. Visibly, Sabrina showed no sign of pain. However, finally her that's-the-way-it-must-be attitude toward pain got the best of her.

When we brought her back to be looked at again, Dr. Bivens couldn't believe Sabrina had been able to walk in her present condition. There was no telling how much damage had been done and how much pain she had endured.

She told us the damage she could see on the X-rays would require another specialist and offered two suggestions. Knowing how we felt about the University of Florida she suggested we take Sabrina back the veterinary school. However, a call to the university determined that it would be two weeks before a surgeon could see her.

Waiting was out of the question as far as I was concerned.

Our second choice was a well-known veterinary surgical hospital in Largo, Florida, over a hundred miles away.

There was one surgeon in particular that Dr. Bivens felt we should see, and fortunately, a call to him netted us an early appointment the next morning.

Armed with X-rays and with Sabrina once again reading road maps and directing traffic from the backseat when she wasn't sacked out sleeping, we made the first of what would turn out to be an eighteen-month series of trips to Largo to repair her leg.

Over the years we have been blessed to find veterinary professionals that love what they are doing, and Dr. Matt Oakes, a board certified member of the American College of Veterinary Surgeons was no exception.

He took a liking to our little girl the moment they met, and although Sabrina did her best Klingon disappearing act every time she saw him, she was never able to cloak herself as she attempted to hide under my chair.

From that first meeting, Matt Oakes always greeted her the same way, "Hey, you," and it was said with nothing but love and concern.

When you work with a university veterinary medical center or a surgical center for that matter, expect to see the worst because that's what you'll find when you arrive.

The folks at Largo were specialists in areas of veterinary medicine that, as before, I didn't know existed. As for their patients, well, if you were a pet lover, at times it could break your heart.

The first thing I noticed were the three-legged dogs. I thought about my little girl and dreaded the possibility of ever having to approve a decision to take a leg, I didn't know if I'd have the courage to do that to her.

I know it sounds silly. You do what you have to do. Yet as I watched those dogs moving about, missing a front or hind leg and apparently making the best of it, my stomach churned. As upset as it left me, my respect for the internal strength of these pets and their desire to survive and make do left me in awe.

Dr. Oakes took Sabrina away for a series of scans and X-rays, and after a thorough exam met with us to go over the results of what he had found and the surgical options available to us.

Blubbering idiot that I am, it took all the strength I could muster to hold back the tears, and even so, the tears began to flow as Dr. Oakes reviewed the scans and explained our options.

"Because Sabrina still believes she's a puppy and there's never anything wrong with her, I'm afraid my first choice will see you back here again."

I hadn't heard him say the leg was going to have to be taken, and that was the good news so we listened as he continued.

"If she wasn't prone to repeat this injury again, I'd suggest we build a new cruciate ligament out of nylon. It's kind of like fishing line, but it's stronger, and it really works.

"However, because Sabrina doesn't seem to know enough to know what she can and can't do, she has a tendency to overdo. I'm afraid she's apt to tear the new ligament, requiring repeated surgeries."

I knew I didn't want to chance putting her through repeated surgeries, so I crossed my fingers and listened intently as he explained the second option.

"The alternative is to realign her bones. She's spent too much time on that leg since the ligament tore, and as you can see from the films, her bones no longer align properly. They'll have to be moved back as close to normal as we can get them. After that I'll secure them in order to give her leg a chance to heal.

"By using a metal plate and screws, I believe we can hold the bones in place. If she's careful over the first several weeks after surgery, the bones and ligament damage will mend, and although she'll walk with her leg turned out a bit, the chances of future problems will be greatly reduced.

"I think that's our best course of action even though her rehabilitation time will be longer.

"You'll have to use a sling to move her in an out of the car and out to do her business until the leg begins to mend and she builds confidence in it. In the long run, if we can position everything properly and you are very careful with her, I think that's the direction to take.

"You need to understand that Sabrina's not a puppy anymore, even though she thinks she is. There are risks during and after surgery, but I'll do everything I can to see that the procedure and her care while she's here recuperating start her on the road to recovery."

We knew she was in good hands. Matt Oakes, like Dr. Barnes and Dr. Ward, was one of those people you like from the moment you meet. We had no doubt that he would take good care of our girl!

"When can you operate and how long will she be here at the hospital?" I asked.

"I'll work her in on today's surgery schedule, but I have no idea what time I'll get to her. I expect she will be with us for several days after surgery for observation and to make sure there's no infection," he responded.

Through the entire discussion Sabrina lay at my feet listening and looking up at me from time to time. Thankfully, she had no idea what was about to happen to her.

For my part, I felt as though a heavy hand had been lifted off my shoulders. My big girl would walk again on all four legs.

Not knowing what to expect when we left home, Carla and I had packed a suitcase. We hugged and kissed our girl and watched as, tail wagging, she followed Dr. Oakes command of "Hey, you," as out the door and back to the surgical waiting area they went.

Once again we were faced with sitting and waiting — waiting and clock watching.

You can only sit and read magazines and books for so long. After a few hours we went out for lunch. Then, it was back to our chairs, where we read, sat, waited, and prayed. On several occasions Matt sent a staff member out to tell us he was running behind due to emergencies.

Finally, we were told he probably wasn't going to get to Sabrina 'til after 7:00 pm. He'd been in surgery all day, but he wasn't going to leave until our big girl's leg was repaired.

We left our motel telephone and cellular numbers with his assistant and asked him to please have someone call us after surgery, no matter what time, to let us know that everything went well.

I'd lost two parents in less than eight months, and suddenly I was experiencing the same sense of sorrow. I found myself visualizing tragedy before I had a reason to be concerned. I know this may sound strange, but then, I guess everyone handles surgical risks in their own way and in their own time.

"She's only a dog," I kept saying to Carla between sobs. "Why am I feeling this way again?"

Yet I knew the answer. They give so much and ask so little. I believe that our pets place their trust in us from the moment we come into their lives. After that, it is what we do with that trust that defines us.

That night, as I lay by the phone waiting for it to ring, I cried and repeatedly talked to God.

I asked him why he was doing this to one of his own, a being that had never hurt anything or anyone.

I even offered to take her place where her after surgery pain was concerned, but that obviously wasn't going to happen.

Finally, after 10:00 pm Matt Oakes called to tell us the surgery was completed and Sabrina was resting comfortably.

He indicated that he'd been able to realign the bones and affix the plate with the screws needed to hold her right leg in place. Now the healing process could begin — the rest was up to Sabrina, God, and time.

We were warned about infection, and he told us he'd get into specifics in the morning.

Dr. Oakes had been in surgery close to twelve hours that day, so we thanked him and agreed to meet the next morning at the Surgery Center.

It sounded as though my little girl was going to be all right. Thank you, God!

Words can't describe the relief that Carla and I felt after that call.

We met with Dr. Oakes the next morning, and he went over everything that had been done. He described the rehabilitation process that Sabrina would have to go through and repeated his request that she remain at the center for observation and initial handling for a few days. After that he said they would show us everything we needed to know and we could take her home.

Knowing how I felt about her, he allowed me to go back to her kennel cage for a quick pat on the head, words of encouragement, a kiss, and promise that we'd be together soon.

The next few days really dragged. We — or more specifically I — called morning, afternoon, and night to get periodic reports on her progress. I may have been a pain in the butt to the surgical staff, but they never let on.

The staff response was always the same. Caring and concerned. Those directly responsible for handling our girl became instant admirers of her disposition and spirit.

She was eating, passing her food, and with the assistance of a sling under her belly, assistants were able to take her for short walks outside.

Initially, she had to stand on three legs to do her business. Slowly they allowed her to put a little weight on her hind leg. The leg was splinted and soft bandaged from her toes to her hip in order to protect it against accidents.

With each trip outdoors, they said she was getting stronger. I wasn't surprised, after all, that was my girl!

I will never understand how God created our pets. To this day, I consider them to be one of his greatest achievements. To me, it seemed as though no matter what is done to them, they have an uncanny ability to bounce back in a matter of days.

Under the same circumstances, we humans would no doubt require weeks, perhaps months, of intensive therapy and rehabilitation, all the while grimacing in pain.

As far as my littlest big girl was concerned, pain was not a word in her vocabulary.

Finally, after what seemed an eternity but was just a few days, we drove up to Largo to bring Sabrina home.

Dr. Oakes went over the latest films, showing us how the plate and screws had been attached. To our surprise, he indicated he could already see regrowth starting to form, and most importantly, there was no sign of infection.

I lost it when I saw the X-rays and the plate and screws that were holding her leg in place. How could anyone, or for that matter any living thing, go through what I was viewing?

When I finally saw her coming down the hall, I don't know who crossed the twenty or so feet between us faster, me on two reasonably good legs or Sabrina on three and in a sling. It was a race to meet, with me getting down on the floor to catch my eighty-pound bundle of joy. As I hugged, stroked, and kissed her, she was busy squealing, crying, and licking my face at a furious pace. As far as she was concerned, all was right in the empire. Surgery, what surgery!

Dr. Oakes showed us the appropriate way to use a large towel as a sling. As he walked her, we headed out to our car. He talked us through everything we had to do when taking her outside, and where to place the sling when lifting her. He wanted us back in little over a week for more films and checks, so I left Carla and Sabrina in the car and went back inside to make an appointment, pay the bill and pick up her new prescriptions. Then we were homeward bound.

We always knew when Sabrina was content. She would stretch her long body out on the backseat, roll on her side, and just sigh. And so it was on this ride.

She may have been in great pain, but we'd never be allowed to know it. As far as my big girl was concerned, we were all back together, and her world was complete.

We stayed in touch with Dr. Oakes by phone, giving him progress reports during the week.

I felt her every step once we got her home and began the rehabilitation process. She was brave. I wasn't. Each step she took as we moved her back and forth to do her business twisted my stomach into knots. When she began placing a little weight on her injured leg, it was as if someone was taking a knife to my heart.

Carla and I had airline reservations to travel to visit our grandkids in Detroit. The twin boys were four years old and beginning to talk up a storm, so you can imagine how anxious we were to see them.

We only saw them once or twice a year and, as the reservations had been made for some time, we really didn't want to cancel our visit if it could be avoided.

However, there was no way we were going to leave Sabrina alone if there was any chance she might damage the surgery.

We discussed the trip at length with Dr. Oakes. Two weeks would pass before we were scheduled to leave. He advised us that if the films taken just before the trip looked good and as long as Sabrina was in the hands of a good boarding kennel he saw no problem with the trip.

The boarding kennel we used on occasion was part of a large veterinary facility. It was new, and the few times we had used them it appeared to be well run.

Doctors were available immediately if there was a problem, so this became a real plus.

I talked to the doctor that owned the facility and brought her Sabrina's complete surgical records. I also went over Dr. Oakes instructions. She said there would be no problem and not to worry about leaving her with them.

As we were only going to be gone from Friday to Monday we decided to take the chance and make the trip.

You could pay for all sorts of extra services for your pup at this boarding kennel, and I did. We made sure that Sabrina would have visits and visual checks several times each day by members of the staff.

I wanted overkill where care was concerned, nothing less would do.

I was assured that her run and sleep area would remain heavily padded throughout her stay and that the boarding staff would sling her for her trips outdoors.

Picking a kennel always leaves you wondering. Do they actually do what they say they will do? Will they follow the instructions you've left for them? Do they check on their charges as often as they say they will when you've paid for extra services? Is your pet getting the right food, treats, and the meds you've left with them at the proper times?

I think you can see where I'm going. I don't care how good the kennel area looks, how well the staff is dressed, or how well trained and caring they claim to be. In the back of your mind there is always that lingering question — are they really taking good care of my baby?

Of course, with Sabrina's other medical problems her current situation simply compounded the issue.

She needed her regular medications, and if she got anxious we'd left meds to settle her stomach down. Missing anything could bring on an attack that might take several days to overcome.

Her last checkup with Dr. Oakes went well. The plate was in place, and the screws holding it were doing their job. It was apparent that new bone growth had taken place, and the medication she was taking to protect against infection was working.

We went over our plan with Dr. Oakes one last time, and he said, "Go. Don't worry. If there's any kind of problem, leave the vet in Port Charlotte my numbers and have them call me immediately."

So with more than a bit of apprehension, we packed our bags, dropped Sabrina off on the way to the airport, and headed north for our visit.

The few days we were gone felt like an eternity. You try your best to have a good time and enjoy each visit with your kids and grandkids, but somehow with our girl back home, alone, and away from us at the moment, I found myself calling the vet's office several times a day.

Each call brought the same response, "She's a love. She's doing just fine. Don't worry. We're on top of everything."

If something sounds too good to be true, chances are it isn't, and in this case — it wasn't!

When we arrived at the vet clinic to pick her up on Monday, our concerns seemed to vanish. At first glance, Sabrina's appearance seemed to correspond with their reports.

I paid the bill, and the three of us headed for the car. As we walked, with Sabrina in a sling between us, I noticed that her right hind leg was out at an angle that was more pronounced than when we'd left her.

I told Carla to stop and carefully switch places with me. I wanted her to see if I was mistaken. I wasn't. What's more, Carla found a large hot spot behind her injured leg, something that should have been easily seen and treated by the vet staff.

When a pup gets anxious and agitated they can, and often do, begin licking parts of their body. They can lick so hard they remove the hair in a given area and then lick their way through the skin with their rough tongues.

The damage they do can be very painful when a wound is open. In this case it not only covered a large area, it was open and ugly.

I was mad. What the hell had the vet staff been doing for three days? We'd been told not to worry. Every time I talked with them on the phone they told me they were on top of everything. Now it appeared they hadn't even spotted something as apparent as a hot spot, much less Sabrina's rear leg at a severe angle.

Once we got Sabrina in to the backseat of the car I went back inside to talk to members of the staff. I might as well have been talking to the blind, deaf and dumb as far as they were concerned.

"Well, I never," and "Gee, how could that happen?" One excuse after another was the best response I could get from the kennel staff. Never once did anyone suggest we bring her back in and at least allow them to clean and treat the hot spot.

I told them they would hear from us again after we determined the extent of Sabrina's physical damage, and although I did manage to elicit a sincere apology from one staff member as I headed out the door, never once in the weeks that followed did the vet that owned the facility call to apologize or to find out how Sabrina was doing.

As soon as we got home, Carla cleaned the wound and treated it with an antibiotic ointment.

Looking back, I should have sued them, but our primary concern at the time was Sabrina.

I've felt for some time that "service and concern for the customer" was a dying art, and I guess this incident proved it. We may not have sued, but I can assure you that Carla and I talked with enough neighbors about that vet and their service to ensure that "word of mouth" did appropriate damage.

Carla called Dr. Oakes when we got home. She described what we were looking at where Sabrina's leg was concerned, and as always, he told us to bring her up the next morning and somehow he would fit her in to his schedule. We did, and the results were a nightmare.

New films showed the plate holding her bones together had split and several screws had broken.

Dr. Oakes was shocked. He said that in all his years of surgery he had never seen anything like this happen. As far as he was concerned, it was a million to one shot.

Later, he talked to the manufacturer of the surgical parts to see if they had been experiencing any malfunctions and was told what he suspected — it just never happened.

Well, it did, and the screws that had broken needed to be removed or, at worst, smoothed down so as not to do more harm.

Much of the broken plate holding her bones would have to be removed. Another plate would need to be added to hold her leg in place once the bones were repositioned.

As if this wasn't bad enough, Sabrina's X-rays showed that she now had a hairline fracture that would require additional time and care in order to heal.

It had been less than a month since her leg surgery, and once again we found ourselves back in a waiting room, registered at a motel, and later that evening waiting by the phone for the results of a second and more delicate operation.

We'll never know if the kennel people didn't sling Sabrina properly, or if by some quirk of fate she managed to get away from her handlers. According to the vet's employees, they'd followed all of our instructions. Yet no one had noticed that her right hind leg was off at a greater angle than when we left her. As for the hot spot, that was a no-brainer unless her handlers were blind.

Calls to the vet center became a waste of time. The staff and the doctor weren't talking. No one had seen or done anything wrong.

Moral of the story, don't take your boarding kennel at their word. Check them continually on everything they say they did when you return from a trip.

If you find they haven't done what they agreed to do, determine whether you are willing to give them another chance. Or better yet, find yourself another boarding kennel. Don't ever allow anyone to needlessly or forgetfully neglect your pet.

Dr. Oakes was able to fit Sabrina in to his surgical schedule and completed the surgery after the close of business.

Once again, we waited by the phone at the motel. Thankfully, the news was good. Well, as good as could be expected. He explained that he had been able to stabilize the bones and minimize the danger from debris and the broken plate.

I'd "gone to the well" one more time where God was concerned, and he hadn't let me down.

Every time I saw a three-legged dog in the Largo waiting room or one with wheels replacing its rear legs, I thanked God for large favors and counted my blessings.

Carla used to say that if anyone else owned Sabrina they probably would have put her down. Not me. As far as I was concerned, we would age together no matter the cost, the problems or the emotional strain.

Arriving at this conclusion seemed second nature to me. Yet, this transformation did not happen overnight. I'd made mistakes in my life, — mistakes that took years to face and understand — and even longer to remedy. Now, I felt as though God was watching — guiding and testing me, making sure that I didn't repeat the same mistakes again.

Ever wonder if pets are the arms of God — reaching out to love us, no matter what? I do!

If waiting for the results of the first surgery was a heart stopper, Sabrina's second surgery left us completely drained.

Several days later, as we waited to collect our child and bring her home, Dr. Oakes told us that we would have to confine her movement even more than before. Yes, we would have to use a sling and keep her on a short leash She was to take no more steps than absolutely necessary when outside to do her business. The same held true when she was in the house. Our job was to make sure that she placed as little weight as possible on her back leg.

The recovery process was truly step-by-step. Watching her move was as painful for me as it was for her. The difference: she never showed it; while I felt her every step!

There would be no trips this time around. We intended to make sure that one of us would always be with her.

The healing process went smoothly. In fact, being eternally optimistic, I began to believe that we were finally over the hill and on a downward path to getting the best we could expect out of Sabrina's now, twice operated on, right hind leg.

I couldn't stop blaming myself for taking the trip to Detroit. In hindsight, no pun intended, if I had it to do over again, we'd have postponed the trip.

With each post surgery visit to Largo, her X-rays showed continuing new bone growth and improvement.

Dr. Oakes was taking no chances with this second surgery. Sabrina's leg was placed in a more solid protective cast in order to minimize any debilitating movement.

You have no idea how good it was to finally hear the words, "I think you've made your last trip up here," from Dr. Oakes.

I'm sure Sabrina couldn't have agreed more!

The thought that maybe, just maybe, my girl was on the way back to being her old self was music to our ears.

Little by little Sabrina put the second surgery behind her, and although I would never again allow her to run with abandon, I was beginning to believe that she could get along in a satisfactory manner without pain for as long as she was with us.

With each month that passed we stretched her walks, walks that had begun with just a few steps and were slowly lengthened. I continued to use a short leash because I knew that the first time she saw a bird or a neighbor she'd want to get to them to say hello. The thought of her taking off with an enthusiastic burst of speed scared the daylights out of me.

If there is such a thing as an overprotective parent, I was it. I wanted Sabrina with me for as long as possible, and I knew we were beginning to approach the outer limits of many shepherds from an age standpoint.

However, no matter how much we tried to protect our four-legged child, when you have an adult dog that thinks it can do everything it did as a puppy and has no fear or concern for pain, sooner or later something is going to happen, and it did.

Carla and I watched over her and at times probably hovered over her — if you were Sabrina and could talk. We were careful. We attempted to control everything she did, but no matter how hard we tried or how cautious we were, we just couldn't take the puppy out of the dog. She was intent upon making the most of every day.

She still brought us toys every time we sat down, and she didn't expect, she demanded that we throw them. We did, but tried to curtail her running by shortening the distance between us.

Nearly a year after rehab once again we began to notice that her right hind leg was beginning to splay outward more than what we now considered normal. I guess sometimes when you are to close to a problem you begin to question yourself and what you are seeing.

Sabrina didn't seem to be favoring it, and as we knew the leg would never be straight this time we watched and waited too long, thinking this was just a natural evolution based upon time, two surgeries and the way she was forced to walk.

It wasn't!

Growing concern finally caused us to make an appointment, and once again the three of us headed for Largo.

The routine was the same, and sadly, as in the past, the X-rays showed that once again, Sabrina's bones had shifted. The plates holding them weren't doing their job!

As usual, Dr. Oakes was confident that he could make the necessary repairs. However, he explained that this third effort was going to be more difficult than the first two.

He said that this time, in order to insure that Sabrina's bones remained stable, he planned to run a rod through her leg. This rod would attach on the outside to more rods that would hold the leg firmly in place. He was taking no chances. This time he intended to make doubly sure that everything was held securely until he was absolutely, positively sure that the healing process was complete. Talk about a medieval torture, this latest solution must have come directly from the middle ages!

Just listening to the description of this device was gut wrenching, but as it turned out, when it rains it pours. The bad news just kept coming.

Sabrina's latest X-ray package showed that time and her tolerance for pain had been working overtime. Years of continuous added pressure on the leg had resulted in significant damage to her spine. She had placed so much strain on her spine as a result of two surgeries and the current damage, that she had ruptured two spinal discs.

Now, I've been through a number of spinal operations over the years. In my case, I face what appears to be a lifetime of visits to the operating table. As a result, I have a great deal of respect for the care one has to take when dealing with the spine after surgery.

Hearing that Sabrina would have to undergo not one but two operations, and knowing the second one would involve her spine, left me with mental pictures of her coming back to me paralyzed.

Paralysis was the fear I faced every time I was on the operating table. The first thing I would do upon waking from surgery was to wiggle my toes to make sure everything was still working. As I thought about Sabrina and what she was about to go through, unable to comprehend fear, much less pain, I felt helpless — my insides were being torn apart — a piece at a time. How much did my child, this beautiful creation of God have to endure in one lifetime? For the first time since coming to us, I felt as though maybe, just maybe, continuing to keep her alive wasn't fair!

Dr. Oakes said that he wanted to do the two surgeries, back to back — no humor intended. Because of Sabrina's age, he felt it best to keep her under anesthetic and get all of his work done at once, rather than subjecting her to a second surgery.

Each surgery represented a high degree of risk. As I listened to Dr. Oakes, I kept asking myself, "how much pain and reconstruction could one small body tolerate?

Talk about asking for miracles — all we could do was wait and pray, and yet, I knew that I had to give her the opportunity to come back to us - knowing full well that her surgery was in excellent and caring hands.

I don't know about Carla, but speaking for myself, I could not understand why God was continuing to place one obstacle after another upon my little girl. After all, wasn't she one of his creations?

I prayed and then I prayed some more. I didn't ask him to relieve the pain and anguish I was feeling. All I asked was that he return Sabrina to me — in whatever form he saw fit and I would love and care for her.

I told him that I would not question his judgment. I hoped that he was still listening!

Life isn't one piece of cake after another. I've learned that over the past ten years and an equal number of surgeries. We can ask ourselves, "why me?" And, I have, but it never seemed to matter. Sabrina, on the other hand, taught me to get up, overcome my pain and move on — and as often as possible, do it with a smile on my face. It's not always easy, but if she could do it, I had to try!

I don't know what was more difficult for me to handle: the repeated surgeries, wondering if this time Dr. Oakes would find that the damage to her leg was surgically impossible to repair, or waiting for word that the surgery was over and a success?

Even now, it is difficult to describe what was going through my mind as we waited in our hotel room — the phone just a reach away. Minutes turned into hours. It was as if I could feel the minute hand on my watch moving ever so slowly. I could hear the second hand counting off the seconds — *tick, tick, tick!*

Sabrina never knew it, but during that period in her life, she had more friends rooting for her than I could have dreamed possible. Over time, she had touched so many people, and everyone wanted to know how she was doing.

Everyone asked about her and was worried about her. As much as she had touched us, she had obviously reached out and captured the hearts of our neighbors and family member's.

As far as my big girl was concerned, she probably considered this latest setback, no big deal — just another bump in the road of life.

"Don't worry" she'd probably say. *"I'll be up and around before you know it, Dad."*

And that's what scared me the most. You just can't explain to a dog that it absolutely, positively has to "slow down and smell the grass." How is it that we humans can "retire" and slow down, yet our pets don't know the meaning of the word?

Once again the phone rang, and thankfully the news was good. Both surgeries had gone well. This time, though, the spinal surgery would complicate our handling of Sabrina during rehabilitation. As careful as we had been in the past, for the next few months we would be walking on eggshells! Too much pressure on the spine while using a sling to help her move about and there was no telling how much additional damage we could do. There was danger every time we moved her.

Sabrina handled both operations with a smile. Cast and bandages aside, when she came down the hall, with Dr. Oakes holding her in a sling, you would have thought that nothing was wrong — that she'd just returned from a vacation. No matter how hard we "wished," she just couldn't get it through her beautifully elongated head just how far she had "pushed the envelope" with this latest round of surgeries.

Everything went well for the first twenty-four hours after we brought her home. Then, out of the jaws of victory came a new challenge.

Carla was sitting and reading. Sabrina was resting on the floor next to her, keeping her company. Carla reached down to pet her and felt something wet. When she drew her hand back it was wet and contained hair. She got down on the floor and gently ran her hand over the same area — more hair came off. Now hair was coming off Sabrina's side in clumps. The hair kept coming off until an eight inch square of raw flesh was exposed, with pus pouring out of the wound.

A quick call to Dr. Oakes, and we were back in Largo waiting for word about our little girl.

When Dr. Oakes came out to talk to us, he indicated it had been necessary to remove more remaining contaminated hair and tissue. He had cleaned the area thoroughly and applied a generous coating of ointment. He gave us a prescription for the ointment he had used, and told us that we would have to keep the affected area clean, treated and open to air.

When we asked him how something like this could have happened he explained that apparently the grounding plate that was used during surgery was responsible for the damage that wasn't seen immediately.

We were told that Sabrina's flesh would need to be treated daily and that the area could not be bandaged. Her body needed air to reach the burned area in order for it to form a scab, heal itself completely, and allow new hair to grow. This may have sounded simple and yet, keeping her off the injured side presented us with another problem.

In her nearly eleven years with us, this was the only time that Sabrina ever acknowledged pain. She allowed Carla to treat the area but not without a gentle nuzzle each time to remind her to be careful.

The healing process would not happen overnight and presented us with a new set of complications. When using the sling, her leg, spine, and the open and raw skin on her side, all could be damaged further and create more pain if we made a mistake when taking her out or simply moving her.

Sabrina's extended rehabilitation provided me with an opportunity to spend more floor time with my child. I would rub and stroke her, and she would take great pleasure in my words and deeds as I told her how important she was and that soon we'd be back together enjoying long walks.

My beautiful child wasn't very beautiful to look at, but as with every obstacle she faced, she did so with the same love and affection we showered upon her.

Sometimes it seemed the trips to Largo for X-rays, surgery and checkups would never end. Finally, with fingers crossed, we were told to bring her up to Largo for what we prayed would be our final visit.

Dr. Oakes announced that the healing process in all areas was complete. The rods were removed from her leg, and the open area on her side and belly was beginning to show new signs of hair growth. He told us there would be no need to return. Oh, but could it be true!

We left hoping that maybe, just maybe, there would be no more doctors in her life — with the exception, of course, of her annual shots.

Sometimes life can involve one curve after another, for humans as well as pets. None of us know what is waiting just around the corner, so, based upon our experiences with Sabrina, the solution seemed clear — make the most of every day and move forward!

For Sabrina, it must have seemed that her life had finally returned to normal. How did I know this? Because when she was stretched out on the tile floor, lying on her side, one of my favorite pastimes involved lying down behind her. I'd wrap my arms around her, give her a bear hug and rub her belly. Within seconds I'd hear a sigh of contentment. Hearing that simple sound was a sign that the world was in its proper orbit.

I know that chances are what I am telling you about our relationship may be a little hard to digest — a bit over the top. After all, she was only a dog — right?

Wrong!

I didn't care who said I was spoiling her, or that dogs should be treated — like dogs. As far as I was concerned, God loaned Sabrina to us in order for me to love and protect her every day she was with us.

He programmed her to be a child with special needs. She was, and as far as I was concerned would continue, to be treated that way for as long as I had the good fortune to have her with me.

Ever since we moved to Florida, time and years seemed to fly by. Just as Sabrina's life was entering a period of elderly bliss, my biggest little girl managed to shake us up again.

She'd enjoyed good health for what to her must have seemed an eternity. During this time, one of our neighbors was having good luck with a lady that came and stayed with their dogs while they were away. They were very pleased with the results.

Dorothy gave us her live-in pet sitter's name, and we met Donna. She was the answer to a prayer. Sabrina liked her immediately, and the feeling was mutual. At last, maybe we could go away for a few days and know that she would be in great hands.

After all, I was the one that had said, "Never again — never would I allow Sabrina to be placed in a boarding kennel after the problems we'd encountered."

Until Donna, Carla, and I had made up our minds that Sabrina would either travel with us on vacations or we would stay at home.

Thanks to Donna, we decided to take a short cruise and would you believe? Everyone got along famously. Sabrina and the cats loved Donna and why not? She spoiled them almost as much as we did!

Finally, Sabrina had the non-stop attention she deserved. Donna was with her morning, noon, and night while we were gone.

The one bad thing about the cruise we chose was the fact that I couldn't reach out by phone too often due to bad connections in Mexico. So, I crossed my fingers and counted the days until we returned home.

As always, every night, I sent telepathic messages to my girl telling her we'd be home soon and not to worry. I told her to sleep well, dream of angels and to have good doggie dreams.

She did just that. She actually enjoyed her new houseguest. So much so that she hardly seemed to care when we arrived back home.

However, not long after the cruise our good fortune where her health was concerned came to an end.

After five operations, including three on her right hind leg and a fourth on her spine, the added weight she placed on her left hind leg finally took its toll.

Fortunately, we knew what signs to look for where her legs were concerned. When we saw her left hind leg beginning to splay out, we made arrangements to see Dr. Oakes.

We knew the routine and were equally sure what we were going to hear.

It came as no surprise when Dr. Oakes told us that Sabrina had torn the cruciate ligament in the left hind leg and would once again need surgery. However, this time his surgical recommendation was different.

"Sabrina's not getting any younger. Because the two of you have always been careful to control her movement, I think it would be best this time if we built a new ligament made of nylon. The life expectancy of the nylon ligament may not be as great as with the plates and screws we used before, but the operation will be less severe. I think she'll tolerate the end result much better. One thing won't change, you can expect the same rehab restrictions as before, after surgery."

Have you cver asked yourself this question about a loved one — "is this the surgery that they won't tolerate? Is this the one that won't have a satisfactory ending?" I had, and I found myself asking those same questions all over again. As far as I was concerned, what Sabrina was going through, time and again, seemed to be obliterating the odds for a safe return — but where life is concerned, you play the cards you are dealt and leave the rest to God and your surgeon.

At this point, whatever Dr. Oakes recommended was just fine with us. Over time we'd come to believe that he would never suggest or do anything that wasn't in the best interest of our girl.

I don't know what was more difficult for me to handle, the repeated surgeries, the continued fear that more damage could be done, or whether this would be the last time she would have to undergo surgery.

Sabrina was back in surgery the next day. The waiting, repair, and rehab was about to begin again.

It is hard for me to describe the mental and physical turmoil I experienced every time Sabrina went under the knife without repeating myself. Each time, I found myself waiting in a motel room. The telephone, just an arms reach away. Every minute seemed an eternity as I listened as the minute hand on my wristwatch moved and the second hand went *tick, tick, tick!*

When Sabrina was released to us, she returned with her tail wagging and her ever present smile overshadowing the pain she must have been feeling. To look at my little girl, you would have thought she'd just returned from visiting a friend — which of course, Dr. Oakes had become.

I wish that I could have greeted her with a smile on my face. I don't know about you, but I'm a softie. I tear up at sad movies and movies with happy endings. Although I should have been elated to see her coming down the hall one more time with Dr. Oakes, I wasn't. Realizing how much she'd been through over the years, I couldn't hold back the tears.

As far as my little girl was concerned as she looked into my eyes, eyes, now red from blubbering, I could almost hear her whispering, "*Don't worry, Dad. I've been here before. Rehab will be a walk in the park!*"

Rehabbing always afforded me with an opportunity to tell her over and over, just how special she was and that before she knew it we'd be playing with her toys and going for walks.

Time is a wonderful healer, and as Sabrina regained her strength, I hoped and prayed once again that she'd made her last visit to Largo. I knew that my time with her was slowly coming to an end, and being greedy, I didn't want to share any of it with doctors. I wanted as much time with her as possible.

God surely does create remarkable creatures. They come to us with an almost "devil may care attitude" as they dazzle us with their goofy antics. They are loyal to a fault, as was the case when Sabrina placed herself in danger by escaping the house to come looking for us as we were out in the harbor, on our boat.

No matter the pain, with a leg in a cast, and moving on three legs or two, our pets still come charging to greet us as if we were a long-lost friend. Whether they've been separated from us for hours or days, their response never changes.

I think I am safe in saying that God works his magic on his children in ways that I will never fully understand.

Hey, Charley, You Don't Scare Me

What was that?

"I'm not sure," I responded.

"Are you thinking what I'm thinking?" Carla asked, with more than a touch of concern in her voice.

For over twenty years the two of us had almost always thought as if we were one, and today would be no different.

"I don't know. Tell me what you're thinking," I said, not wanting to be the first to say what thoughts were racing through my mind.

"We're going to die!"

When you move to Florida, depending upon where you choose to live, the potential for disaster, the result of a hurricane, is always tucked in the back of your mind.

In our case, we had three strikes against us.

First, we lived on the Gulf of Mexico side of Southwest Florida.

Second, we were on a canal created inlet/outlet to Charlotte Harbor, a twenty-plus-mile waterway that leads to the Gulf of Mexico. We were less than three miles from a large and very warm body of water.

Third, and equally important, our home was in a primary flood area. Should a hurricane hit, and if it brought with it a storm surge, the fact that our house was just ten feet above sea level meant we could well be history.

On the plus side, our area hadn't been hit in over thirty years, so although everybody talked about hurricanes during the season — June to November, most of us believed that it would never happen to us.

Every year we watched, waited, and made plans to evacuate if there was even the slightest chance that a hurricane coming up the Gulf Coast would hit anywhere near us.

Near, really didn't have to mean direct or even close. The radius of a hurricane can extend more than a hundred miles. This meant that even if the eye didn't pass over us, the outer bands could still bring high winds and heavy rains. We found that out two months after we moved here.

For six years we'd evacuated when necessary, or rolled the dice, closed the storm shutters, and sat out the not-so-near misses. We'd been lucky. Others, to the north and south of us, on the east coast of Florida, and in the western Gulf hadn't been so lucky.

Two thousand four was no different than prior years. The "watch" began in June and would last through the end of November.

However, this year would be different. Today was Friday, August the 13th. Superstitious?

For Sabrina, it was just another day. Eat, sleep, poop, and dispense love from dawn 'til bedtime, fully expecting to receive payment in kind from anyone she came in contact with. The only difference, she still had her leg in a cast.

I can't say that I remember everything that happened leading up to "Charley." However, I can tell you that we started out feeling confident of another miss and ended up praying for our lives!

We'd been watching Charley as she grew in size and moved ever so erratically toward the Florida coastline. As it got within thirty-six hours of us, its path was projected to be well to our south — nothing to worry about.

Next morning, the path and projections had Charley moving up the coast toward Tampa. That still had us in the outer edges of the storm. That meant plenty of rain and wind, but no reason to pack up and leave.

A neighbor on our cul-de-sac was an active member of the coast guard auxiliary, both on the water and in the air. He'd placed a radio tower alongside his house with antennas and wind instruments at the top. Based upon what he was hearing, he was confident we could ride out the outer edges of Charley, which at the time was only a category two hurricane.

Armed with this information and the fact that it had been roughly thirty years since our area had taken a direct hit, we were confident that we'd be safe. We decided to follow the leader. As for the rest of our immediate neighbors, most were either up north dodging Florida's summer heat or had already packed up and evacuated.

The five of us that remained had double and triple tied our boats securely to pilings, ground anchors, and trees in the event that we took even a partial hit from Charley.

We checked boats left behind by neighbors that had evacuated, as well as those that were up north for the summer. Everyone had secured their boats knowing it was hurricane season. However, we wanted to make sure the boats were secured properly and if not, add or tighten lines while there was still time.

The five of us agreed to take the handheld radios we used for backup on our boats inside with us. This way, we could check each other every few minutes to make sure everyone was safe. If we caught the head, tail, or outer edges of Charley and someone needed help, somehow we'd get to them.

We agreed that the radios would be left on for as long as the batteries held. Should anyone have an emergency they could call for help immediately.

We should have known that this Friday wasn't going to be like every other. Remember, it was Friday the 13th!

Who is afraid of the "big, bad wolf?"

We were. Charley kept shifting and moving, moving and shifting again, she couldn't seem to make up her mind who she wanted to batter!

Suddenly, in the last hour Charley changed direction again. Now she was coming right at us. Punta Gorda was about to become ground zero.

Well, so much for confidence!

We'd packed our two cars with most everything we needed to protect: financial records, all checks and account information from the computers, insurance policies, personal documents, water, extra gas for the cars, and of course, clothing. You did this automatically prior to a potential evacuation, even if it looked like it was going to be a near miss.

Our house had been shuttered for a couple of days with only the last of the storm panels needing to be placed at the front door, thus enclosing the house completely, whether we left or stayed.

There's something about living inside a fully shuttered house that causes my imagination to run wild. I liken it to living inside a tomb.

We were told that our storm shutters would withstand over two-hundred-mile-per-hour winds — that was the good news.

The bad news caused us to be concerned — we were sure that our twenty-year-old tile roof wouldn't stand a chance under severe wind conditions.

Punta Gorda Isles had a roof ordinance. All roofs had to be tile. No one knew whether the tile would remain in place during a heavy storm — they just had to be tile!

We were sure that if extremely high winds ever got under the roof tiles there was a good chance the tiles would become shrapnel. Once they became airborne, any unprotected windows, boats, or cars left behind would be fair game.

As if that wasn't enough to worry about, there are always those last minute items that you suddenly remember must go with you. Sadly, you forgot to pack them, and sadder still, now that you need them, you can't put your hands on them. More time wasted looking. If you were hoping to beat a hurricane and make a last minute retreat you didn't stand a chance.

So here we were, with less than an hour's notice. We'd just been advised that Charley was headed directly for Punta Gorda, not Tampa, and that it was no longer a category two hurricane; it was gathering strength and was expected to be a category four when it reached land.

Carla, Sabrina, and I had no choice but to stick it out and hope that Charley suddenly stalled or made another course correction.

Even if we left now, we probably wouldn't be able to outrun the hurricane. Roads were at a standstill due to last minute departures, and the last place you want to find yourself was sitting in your car facing down a hurricane.

Realizing that we had to stay, we made some last minute calls to family on the east coast, telling them that we had no choice but to stay. We told them we hoped this wouldn't be our last goodbye and made preparations to protect ourselves, Sabrina, and the cats.

Three of the houses in our area, including ours, were built either before or immediately after Andrew. That meant none of them were built to codes that would enable them to withstand a direct hit. These houses didn't meet the new Miami-Dade hurricane guidelines, and even if they did, there was no guarantee they'd still be standing after a direct hit from a category four or five hurricane. Projections and calculations are just that in a real world situation — an educated, best guess.

Our house and the one directly across the canal from us were built in the mid-eighties, not a very confidence-inspiring thought. Faced with no other choice but to stay, all we could do was make the best of a bad situation; then pray!

With little time to think, I remembered that the safest place during a hurricane was one where you had four walls and no windows, preferably within the walls of the house, rather than against an outer wall.

We placed the cats in their carriers and moved them into the laundry room, just off the garage. No windows and well inside the four outer walls.

As for Carla, Sabrina, and I, we had one choice; my walk-in closet for the same reason as the laundry room, at least we'd be inside three and a half walls that were protected in part by the outer walls of the house.

However, we'd incorporated built-in shelves in the closets after we bought our house. As a result this left us with less than sixteen broken up feet to accommodate the three of us.

We moved as much clothing as possible to Carla's closet. It was directly across from mine, but on an outside wall. I figured that worst case, the loss of clothes was no great loss.

Then we quickly practiced squeezing into this very small area. It was a tight squeeze. We'd taken: pillows, blankets, a battery operated AM radio, flashlights, lanterns, extra batteries, water, a first-aid kit, and a handheld ship to shore radio with us. If anybody took a deep breath things would get even tighter, but what the hell — at least we were all together.

Like everything else in her life, Sabrina thought that all of us crowding into the closet was a game. She loved the togetherness part of it. Happily, she would follow instructions. Little did she know that for several hours the closet would be her new home.

I took her out to do her business and told her this was the last time — not that she understood. We had no idea when or if she would be able to go out again and we could only pray that her much admired bladder of steel wouldn't let us down. As soon as she was back inside, we replaced the shutters that allowed us to move in and out, and began the wait.

Once the storm hit it would be impossible to take her out no matter how badly she needed to go. Of course, if she did have to go, or for that matter if we did, the thought was not very appealing.

The hurricane information coming over our AM radio indicated we were less than a half hour from the outer edge of the storm. It was time to move into the closet to wait.

When you know a category four hurricane is bearing down on you, the silence while you wait is deafening. As the minutes tick by, don't let anybody kid you, your concern moves to apprehension, and then turns to fright.

I'd heard or read comments made by people that had survived hurricanes, and I can say without reservation, no words do justice to the experience.

Little by little we began to hear the wind picking up. We double checked our radios, and everyone was in protected areas. So we signed off.

Our closet had a bi-fold wooden door with horizontal slats — not very secure. We held the door open as long as we could for ventilation. Once we heard the winds strengthening, the door would have to be closed.

Carla threaded Sabrina's leash through several of the slats in an effort to hold the doors closed. As for us, we propped our feet and pillows against the doors in an effort to keep Charley out — how's that for optimism?

Sabrina was curled up, resting with her head on my lap. Suddenly she began looking around and up at the ceiling. That reaction told us it was time to pray.

Before we knew it, Charley's outer band winds made themselves known. We knew what was next!

That noise that Carla had heard and her earlier question brought the reality of the situation into focus.

"What's that sound?" she had asked.

The sound she was hearing sounded like several freight trains beginning to roll over the top of us, all at the same time.

I will never forget the fear coursing through my body and the fact that I had failed to pay heed to an old sailor's truism when it comes to the weather, "Don't mess with Mother Nature. Get the hell out of Dodge!"

From this day forward, I would remember the sounds and the silence. The blue sky before and after Charley left, and most of all, I would remember the fear!

This time I answered Carla, "I think that's either our roof or the entire house starting to come apart."

And what sounds they were. The groans and creaking grew louder as our house seemed to shake against the wind. Sabrina, our ever present protector, started growling. She may not have known what was happening, but she was ready and willing to take on anyone or anything that tried to harm us, even with a cast on one leg.

I don't know if you've ever heard a German shepherd in full attack mode. We used to joke that when she growled you could feel the floor shake. That wasn't necessary now; the house was already shaking, but as the noise increased, so did her growl.

I suspect this was her way of telling us, "*Don't worry, Mom and Dad, I'll protect you!*"

Sabrina wanted out of the closet. She was ready to tear into whatever she thought was tampering with her house. It was all we could do to hold the door closed and hold on to her at the same time. This was no time for bravery.

It sounded as if the three of us were in a can and someone was beating against it with a baseball bat. *Thump, thump, thump!*

Deep down, I knew that what I was hearing were pieces of our neighbor's homes, pool enclosures, and anything that wasn't tied down bouncing off our house and our storm shutters.

For what seemed an eternity, but was probably little more than thirty minutes, the front of the hurricane passed directly overhead. We just didn't know it at the time!

I'd been through three earthquakes while living in California — one that measured in excess of seven on the Richter scale. The sound and feeling as the ground seems to be moving around and under you, is an experience that stays with you — forever.

However, I can think of nothing that I can compare to the pure fright of believing you are about to die as everything around you sounds as if it is coming apart.

The pressure from Charley was so strong that it burst the batteries in my handheld radio while I was transmitting and acid leakage burnt my fingers. Now we could hear our two neighbors, but were unable to transmit.

It was extremely hot sitting in the closet until a small ceiling panel that provided access to the attic was sucked up and into the attic. Suddenly there was a rush of cool air. As we looked up, we could see light coming from what was left of the roof.

There was nothing we could do but wait and pray, and believe me, when the walls seem to be flexing and your house sounds as though it's falling in on you you're as close to heaven or hell as you ever want to be.

Our little neighborhood of five had checked in a couple of times during the initial hit, and although everyone was scared, we were all still safe.

Then, there was silence. It was as if time itself had stopped.

We didn't realize it at first, but now we were in the eye of the hurricane. Winds were ahead of us. Winds were behind us. For a brief period of time there was an eerie silence.

I opened the closet door a crack, looked around and found that the bedroom was still there. I couldn't say the same for what I could see of our master bath. Later we concluded that the skylight in the ceiling was the door by which Charley entered our house.

Water spots were beginning to form on several areas of the bedroom ceiling, but I didn't see any immediate damage.

As you might expect, Sabrina wanted to be the first one out of the closet. No matter how we tried to hang on to her she was bound and determined to protect us. If anyone was out there she intended to have a piece of them.

Depending on the speed of a hurricane, and fortunately Charley was moving fast, you can have from several minutes to an hour or more before the tail of the storm comes crashing down upon you, and if you're really unlucky, bringing storm surge with it.

We decided to gamble and quickly check the house for damage. What we saw inside left us breathless. We had no idea what had happened to the outside of the house, but inside, one end, was a mess. The ceilings were down, insulation and wires were hanging everywhere and the only thing between the rafters and where the roof once was, was blue sky.

We found a spare leash in the laundry room, having left Sabrina's other leash back on the closet door. We hooked her up in order to satisfy her need to stay as close to us as possible and began to move slowly, fearing that there were nails or other sharp objects on the floor that could harm her.

As best I could tell Charley had blown out the skylight in our master bathroom, just a few feet from where we were huddled in the closet. Having gained entry, she tore through the house. With no unprotected windows or doors available to use for escape, thanks to our storm shutters, Charley exited by blowing out the ceilings and roof at the opposite end of the house.

After a quick inspection, Carla decided to hold Sabrina back in the bedroom while I checked the laundry room and went out to the garage to look for more damage.

The laundry room had come through without a scratch. As for the cats — they were resting calmly in the carrier beds, acting as if nothing had happened.

The garage was a different story. A portion of the inner roof had fallen down onto both of our cars. What hadn't fallen was hanging by a thread.

A large portion of the cattery roof was gone. Our cattery cages were covered with drywall and soggy insulation material. Thank God we had moved the cats to the laundry room.

One side of my office ceiling was gone; the rest was sagging. The ceiling and insulation had fallen in on bookshelves and buried my computers and office equipment.

Model boats that once stood on shelves were destroyed, along with papers and books, as rain poured in through the exposed ceiling.

Of all the rooms, our dining room was the only one that had escaped damage.

We'd taken in considerable water during the first phase of the storm. Not being able to see the outside of the house, and knowing Charley wasn't finished with us yet, we had no intention of venturing outside for a look.

Your first inclination after the front side of a hurricane is to salvage anything you can and prepare for the next hit. The last thing you want to do is find yourself caught in the open when the tail of a hurricane comes through.

Besides, going outside would have meant taking off protective panels on the outer doors-panels that would have to be put back up quickly if we got caught outside as Charley returned.

During prior storms we'd found that rain made the panels slippery and hard to handle. Trying to secure them in any kind of wind and rain was like trying to hold on to the wrong end of a knife with very sharp blade. Because the panels bent back and forth as you tried to hang them, your hands ended up a bloody mess. As far as I was concerned, there would be plenty of time for inspection after the storm had passed. Besides, we couldn't do anything about the damage.

I'd checked my watch when we exited the closet, and not knowing how long it would be before the backside of "Charley" hit us, decided that we should return to the closet.

Once back inside the shelter of the closet we began to think about what we'd just experienced and worried about what Charley's return would bring.

There was still some radio chatter about where and how the storm was moving. Storm watchers were warning everyone within reach of their voice that there was more on the way and not to let their guard down.

Miraculously, if there was a blessing in all this madness it was the fact that Charley was in a hurry. The weather people on our transistor radio reported that Charley was traveling twenty miles per hour — extremely fast for a hurricane. This meant that we weren't going to be in the equivalent of a mix master for hours.

The winds wouldn't linger and beat the hell out everything in sight. Charley would just run over us a couple of times and move on.

So far, the three of us had come through the storm without a scratch. That eased some of our concerns, until we were reminded on the radio that Charley wasn't through with us.

Although dust and minor debris had fallen in on us, so far my closet had provided much-needed protection.

Slowly the clock kept ticking as we waited for the backside of Charley. When you think you are going to die, and you don't, waiting for someone to pull the trigger a second time doesn't provide much comfort. We knew the worst wasn't over, we just didn't know how bad the tail of the hurricane would be or how long it would last.

Then, there was the question of storm surge following the tail of a hurricane. We were only ten feet above sea level, and our canal was about a mile from the harbor if you drew a straight line. As far as the local experts were concerned, if we were hit with a serious surge there was a good chance we would not survive!

We couldn't see what was happening in the canals outside during our short trip through the house. We didn't know if we were on the verge of being swept under water by storm surge. All we could do was look around and confirm that so far, no news, in the form of water rushing across the floors was good news.

During the lull we heard a distress call. A neighbor heard us checking in periodically and was trying to reach anyone that could hear him.

All of us could, but based upon his problem, which was medical, our next door neighbor, Mark, a retired doctor, took the call.

Apparently, the emergency caller had been standing in front of a sliding glass door wall watching as Charley came in.

Not a very good idea.

Well, Charley did just that; she came rushing through his house. Before our unidentified neighbor had a chance to move to safety, his windows were blown in and a flying shard of glass had cut an artery in his arm. He was bleeding badly and facing death if he didn't get help, and he knew it.

Mark talked him through what he needed to do, and several days later, we found out that although the gentleman in question ended up spending ten days in the hospital after Charley, Mark's quick reaction and instructions probably saved his life.

Finally, what seemed forever, but wasn't, the backside of Charley caught up with the three of us as we huddled together in the closet.

We listened as more of the house departed and more of the surrounding homes used our house for target practice and vice versa.

We kissed and said our goodbyes for the second time — just in case! There was only one being in the closet that didn't seem overly worried, Sabrina. For a dog whose body had all but shut down when moving and now, with a splint on her hind leg, seeing her house being torn apart seemed to bring out the best in her. She was alert and ready to take on anyone that dared open the closet door. That — was my little girl!

People who have been through a hurricane will tell you that it's at times like these that your life flashes before your eyes. For us, this was as close to a near-death experience as we ever want to encounter.

Finally, the silence returned. The backside of Charley had passed over us and was gone.

As far as the broadcaster on the radio was concerned, Charley had moved out of the area, leaving a path of destruction in its wake as it headed through the Isles, downtown Punta Gorda and on into Port Charlotte.

Once again, we opened the closet door, hugged each other, tethered Sabrina to a wooden rod in the closet, told her to be a good girl, and headed for the garage. We exited through the side door and removed enough panels on the front door to allow both light and a more convenient exit.

The three houses had come through Charley safely, albeit with varying degrees of damage, ours being the worst.

It was time to face reality. I'm not sure which is worse, the hurricane or your first real look at the damage that's been done. One minute you are praying for your life, and the next, you were looking at a lifetime of savings and hard work that's been torn apart. Charley may have been gone, but the heartache was just beginning.

We didn't know it at the time, but later when our coast guard affiliated neighbor found what was left of his radio tower, the wind indicator on top had broken at 157 miles per hour. Charley had apparently passed directly over us.

We had just come through a category five hurricane, and although badly broken and shaken, we were all alive and able to talk about it.

Of course, that wasn't saying much for our neighborhood. Electrical lines for as far as we could see were down and either lying across the roads or on lawns.

Telephone and street light poles were bent or broken like matchsticks. Those that weren't, were down completely. Street signs had been blown away, leaving many of us wondering how anyone would be able to find us.

Without electricity it didn't take long to discover that water and the pump stations for sewage were out of commission.

When the experts tell you to have plenty of bottled water on hand during hurricane season, and to fill your bathtubs with water, they know what they are talking about.

None of us could even begin to guess when any of the facilities you take for granted would be back up and operating. As it turned out, we lived without the basics for the better part of two weeks.

As I looked at the outside of our house, I could see that most of our tile roof was gone. We were down to bare wood and in some places, no wood at all.

The storm shutters had done their job. They'd taken several hits from flying debris, yet they had remained secure throughout the entire storm.

Carla finally allowed Sabrina out of the closet. She wanted to be with us wherever we went, however, having seen our front lawn, it was obvious that this wouldn't work until we could clear a path through the debris.

With hot electric lines, broken glass, nails, and sharp objects everywhere, it was obvious that her ability to move around outside was going to be very limited for a while.

When you look around and it appears someone has dropped a bomb in your neighborhood the last thing that comes to mind is — *What, do I do first?*

All of a sudden a sense of relief seemed to envelop us. We hugged, kissed and held each other tightly — it was a "group hug" moment. Our little girl had been brave, beyond belief. And, as our bodies and minds caught up with each other, we took a moment to thank God for looking after us.

Next, we hugged our neighbors and cried together.

There is no shame in crying, and during the next several days we cried and then cried some more!

Suddenly you realize that although you may have just lost your largest single possession, you are still alive and that, my friend, is all that counts. Houses can be rebuilt!

You are in shock — you just don't realize it. So you keep moving and checking and looking for things to keep your mind occupied.

Having checked out the front of the house, I went out back to see how that portion of the roof, lanai, pool cage, and our sailboat, *Solitude*, had faired.

The roof at the back of the house was a mess. The gable over our family room was destroyed!

Our lanai roof was all right, but much of the screening was torn apart.

There wasn't much left of the pool cage. Most of it had fallen into the pool.

As for *Solitude*, one look told me she was destroyed. Picture this: her forty-five-foot aluminum mast was bent into a U with the top of the mast buried in over eight feet of water.

Metal rigging was mangled, rails were bent or pulled from the deck, and those neighborhood roof tiles I mentioned earlier, well, what didn't hit our house hit our boat. The entire fiberglass hull and cabin looked like it had been bombed by flying missiles.

For that matter so had my neighbor's boat across the way. Steve had left his roller furled jib on and lashed down, but that didn't stop the wind. By the time Charley was through with his boat, the jib looked like fifty small pennants fluttering in the breeze. The rest of his thirty-five-foot sailboat didn't look much better.

Steve, Cindi, and Steve's mom had left early in order to get away from the threatening storm. When they returned they couldn't believe their eyes.

Tiles from surrounding roofs, no doubt including our own, had gone through their unprotected sliding glass wall of French doors. This wall of windows, or what was left of it, faced the canal from their family room. Once Charley got inside the house, it picked up their furniture and drove it through the house, out the front door and onto their front lawn.

The inside of their house looked as though a giant mix-master had violently stirred everything inside. It was a shambles. Broken glass was everywhere, along with piles of glass that had been reduced to dust by Charley.

Days after they came home, Steve and I stood in our driveway talking about the storm, and before we knew it, we were both crying.

Our canals were littered with aluminum from pool cages that had been ripped away from houses and set sail.

With a trailer park just two canal blocks to the east of us, well, let's just say that assorted clothing and pieces of several trailers were now either residents in our canals, attached to what was left of our houses or resting in our pools and yards.

We had no idea how the rest of the Isles had fared, but from what we could see for several blocks, we were sure that once we were able to move about, the sight wouldn't be pretty.

Days later, we found out that our little downtown historical district had been all but leveled.

Historical homes along and within a few blocks of the riverfront were destroyed by wind, rain and water. Charlotte Harbor had overflowed its banks and left downtown partially under water. Fortunately, it had never reached us!

The two hotels along the river suffered varying degrees of damage. Months later it was determined that one would be repaired and the other had to be demolished.

In reality, those of us that had stayed had been lucky. Although the Peace River overflowed its banks, Charley failed to bring with it the surge that a short time later hit and destroyed so much of the Gulf Coast.

Our little town, Punta Gorda, suddenly became famous. All of the TV networks converged on us to cover the damage.

Up until Charley, I'd read stories about the survivors of hurricanes. I felt sorry for them, but from this day forward I would forever feel and appreciate the shock and mental trauma that would stay with them forever.

There are many stories that took place during the next two weeks, far too many to tell. One of the funniest dealt with our everyday hygiene.

When the water we had saved in the tub in our second bathroom ran out, we used water from our swimming pool to fill and flush toilets. The electric pumps that managed city sewage disposal were down, and it didn't take long before the lines were blocked, but when you've gotta go, you gotta go — so we did!

After washing out of a bucket for several days and brushing our teeth using as little bottled water as possible, there's nothing like a shower, even a cold one.

The island on our cul-de-sac had an underground watering system thanks to the city. The pipes must have burst, and the sprinkler system was doing a fair imitation of Old Faithful as it sent a continuous flow of water into the air.

After several days of looking at it, we gathered under that waterfall in bathing suits or shorts, and with bars of soap in hand, turned Old Faithful into a shower!

Would You Believe?

I will be forever understanding of what people that are hit by a hurricane or other natural catastrophes face insofar as their insurance companies are concerned.

Stonewalling became the order of the day. Suddenly small print in policies that most of us never read was front and center. Insurance companies and their adjusters made an extra effort and took every opportunity to offer less than the coverage provided under the terms of a policy. When these tactics didn't work, there were the outright lies!

Sabrina, with a history of not being able to handle stress, continued to respond remarkably well. Suddenly she was living with us in the one room in the house that remained dry — our dining room. Her house was falling apart before her eyes. Trips to take care of business were done in a very confined area. As far as walks were concerned, they were out of the question. If there ever a moment when God was watching over my little girl, it was now, for even if we needed a vet, there was no way we could get to one!

No thanks to our insurance company, we spent nearly two weeks waiting for and fighting with insurance adjusters, and even then we'd settled absolutely nothing!

As it turned out, our insurance adjuster made several trips to our house before providing us with what the insurance company considered to be a reasonable — and as they called it — final estimate.

While we waited, it rained and rained and rained some more. The more it rained the more our house came apart. One by one all but the dining room ceiling fell in.

Mold began to form on the exposed rafters and began to spread.

Sabrina watched as her house came apart, piece-by-piece. Miraculously, her stomach remained in check.

We managed to get most of our furniture up on bricks and covered with plastic, so it was saved.

We moved our futon from the family room into the dining room before the ceiling fell in. The dining room was the only area that remained dry. It served as our bedroom for two weeks.

I have no idea what was going through Sabrina's mind during that two weeks we were held captive by insurance adjusters. Water logged ceilings collapsed. Kitchen cabinets pulled away from their walls. Continuous rain weighed down what was left of ceilings, insulation, and drywall throughout the house, until they finally succumbed.

If she had an anxiety attack we'd have to deal with it as best we could. For several days there was no way to reach our vet by phone or car. Realizing this, we increased her meds, hoping they would keep her stomach in check.

If traveling from Tennessee to Florida and being left with boarding kennels brought on extreme bouts of anxiety, there was a good chance that Sabrina's stomach was in turmoil. Yet she never showed it. Her ever-present smile was the first thing that greeted us in the morning and the last thing we saw before we went to sleep with her on the floor next to us.

The house leaked like a sieve. We borrowed every spare bucket in the neighborhood, and still we couldn't keep up with the water that was pouring through openings in the roof and ceilings.

Our neighbors across the street, Manny and JoAnne, had very little damage on the outside of the house, save for the fact that they had lost some roof tiles.

We checked the inside of their house to make sure it was dry. When we were finally able to communicate with them in New Jersey, we explained the damage that had been done and that for the most part their home was in good shape.

They decided not to come down immediately, but when they heard what had happened to us, they told us to move into their house and store whatever we could salvage from our house and garage in their empty garage.

We opted to stay in our house with Sabrina, but moved the cats across the street. This was a perfect example of feline flexibility. Cats can live anywhere as long as they have food, water and a clean little box. Thank you, lord. Carla was able to set up portable cages and provide them with a clean, safer environment, and the two of us made frequent visits so that they never felt forgotten.

If there was a silver lining in this horror story, it was one of our living room walls.

A few years earlier we'd begun to collect numbered lithographs by a French painter, Fanch.

Picture this. A dozen framed lithographs hung on one long wall in the living room. A category five hurricane rips our house apart, and not one lithograph moved from its position on the wall. Not one was damaged in any way. Strange, real strange!

Although we lived in the equivalent of a tent with multiple holes in it for two weeks, insurance adjusters couldn't be bothered to come out in the rain to shoot pictures and complete their estimates. Poor babies, they were afraid they might get their feet wet.

When they finally did get their work done, their estimates were an absolute joke! Whatever stories you've heard about used car salesmen — double it! "Sign here. She's a beauty. Have you back up and running like a top in no time." Right!

Fortunately, most of us with major damage had retirement funds, and if we had to use them to fight for what was right where our insurance companies were concerned, then fight we would — and did.

As for our insurance coverage, we learned a hard lesson: read all the small print and force your agent to explain anything you don't understand.

The big print said we were covered for living expenses until our house was rebuilt.

The small print said we were only covered for twelve months. What's more, the start date was the date of the storm. The fact that we couldn't get off the Isles, much less down our street for several days because the roads were impassable, didn't count. As far as they were concerned, it was our job to find a place to live — immediately after Charley departed!

Add to this the fact that initially we didn't dare leave the house for fear of missing our insurance adjusters, and you can see where the two weeks went. You never knew if or when they were going to show up. Times promised meant nothing!

Miss them and there was no telling when they would return — they had a captive audience. Our days of coverage were shrinking fast, but they didn't care.

During that two-week period, our little group of neighbors didn't wait for the National Guard, FEMA, the Red Cross, or any other government body to step in and offer assistance. To us, the disaster that had destroyed our little corner of the world was personal.

We came together and went house to house pulling and piling debris on empty lots nearby.

Since moving to Florida I'd been averaging a spinal operation every twelve months, so heavy lifting was out of the question.

A relative of Ed and Jane, our coast guard neighbors, managed to bring a truckload of building materials from the Miami area.

I'm not very handy with tools, but Carla is, so she spent several days up on the roof nailing four by eight sheets of plywood over exposed areas. Then she covered the plywood with plastic sheeting, all in an effort to keep the rain out. Even with neighbors helping, she fought a valiant but losing battle.

As fast as she covered an area with wood and plastic, nightly rain and winds would rip it away, but she never gave up.

My time was spent bagging wet insulation. I couldn't believe the amount of insulation that had to be bagged and dragged to our dump area. When I wasn't bagging insulation, I was carting pieces of drywall and aluminum from damaged houses.

Surprisingly, as fast as we moved the aluminum into a pile, the next morning it was usually gone. Once roads were partially open, moonlight scavengers "cruised" neighborhoods after dark looking for anything they could take to a scrap yard and sell. Later, we read that one young couple sold enough scrap aluminum to put a down payment on a house.

Once we were able to use our roads, we met with FEMA personnel at a tent site they'd set up not far from us. I know the stories you've read about FEMA, but as far as we were concerned, they were quite helpful. They worked with us to fill out the necessary forms and responded a lot quicker than our insurance company.

The National Guard came through like champs with ice, water, and tarps. I don't know what Sabrina and the cats would have done without them as little by little our supply of drinking water shrunk.

The Guard even had food available if we needed it. All you had to do once the roads were open was drive to the staging area, tell them what you needed, and they would load your car.

No matter where we went, Sabrina was always with us, and everyone had a pat on the head for her. She responded with the usual licks and tail wags.

After the storm, we had no cellular service. I tried and tried but couldn't get a line out. For that matter, nobody could.

Finally, the second day, after several tries, I managed to get a short call to my son in Detroit. I told him we were okay and to call my sister on the east coast of Florida. He needed to tell her that if they could get through they needed to buy us a generator, bring gas, buckets, and cleaning materials.

Somehow Sue and Dan managed to make it all the way across the state. It took them quite a while as roads everywhere were a mess. When they got to Punta Gorda they found that all of the street signs were down, making it even more difficult to get to us, but they did.

With the help of our neighbors, we had our new generator assembled, cranked up, and providing electricity to our freezer and refrigerator.

We even had a few lights working.

Our next-door neighbor ran extension cords from his freezer to our generator, and we provided power for him as well.

The next big problem was fuel to power the generators.

All of the service stations in the immediate area were either destroyed or without power. So once again, everyone stepped up and came together. We took turns driving forty miles to the nearest gas station we could find, to fill up gasoline cans for everyone in the neighborhood.

With generators running around the clock, day after day, gas runs became an almost daily occurrence.

A former neighbor who had moved back to Colorado loaded his motor home with generators, fuel, and everything he could think of that we might need and drove back to Punta Gorda to distribute his load. When anyone asked how much they owed him, his answer was, "Nothing."

Now that's a great neighbor!

Months later Carla and I, and Sue and Dan reversed roles as a hurricane heading for the east coast came on shore. Now we were their support system, setting up insurance support, and helping in any way that we could. Needless to say, knowing what we had experienced, they had already purchased a generator and supplies — just in case.

For some reason, whenever you read about a major hurricane, you also read about dogs and cats that are left behind to fend for themselves. I've never been able to understand this.

The idea of leaving Sabrina and the cats behind had we chosen to try and outrun Charley was out of the question — it never entered our minds. They weren't just pets; they were members of our family and entitled to every ounce of protection we could provide.

You wouldn't leave a child behind to fend for itself, so why leave a pet behind? They give so much and ask so little. Yet in this instance they are often considered disposable by some owners.

As an aside to this story, one of our neighbors adopted a "hurricane" dog several months after Charley. The dog had either been tied up or simply left behind by his owners — owners that never returned for him!

It took more than a few years for that pup, now named Charlie, to feel comfortable around men. In his mind a man had apparently been responsible for leaving him to face Charley alone.

One of the highlights of Sabrina's hurricane experience, if you can call it that, took place a few days after Charley hit.

Afraid that we would lose a considerable amount of meat in our refrigerator, we invited our neighbors over for a driveway barbeque. We supplied the meat, others brought salad, soft drinks, and bread — items that would spoil if they weren't eaten.

One neighbor brought two sawhorses and a four-by-eight sheet of plywood to use as a table. It seated fourteen of us.

Another neighbor brought candelabras, candles, and a white tablecloth. Why not? It was party time!

So there we sat. Good food, wine and good friends. As we dined, an announcer on the radio was telling us that the Red Cross was working their way back to our end of the Isles to see if we needed help. We didn't; we took care of ourselves. More importantly, we looked after each other. Sabrina didn't know who to lick first and her tail never stopped wagging

As for the Red Cross, they never showed.

Just goes to prove, if you want something done, do it yourself.

The afternoon of our party Sabrina was in her element. Neighbors that had stayed behind, and a few that had somehow managed to return, were lavishing her with hugs, kisses, and loads of praise. That tail of hers never stopped moving!

Days later, our neighbor directly across the street told us they had heard that North Port, a city about twenty miles north of us hadn't been hit. With a few roads finally open, Diane, Paul, Carla and I went out to dinner. After living with a propane grill for days and eating off paper plates, the dinner and the time we shared was a real treat.

From what we were reading in the local paper, once we were able to get one, insurance adjusters were running around town waving checks at homeowners, hoping they'd grab them up.

The story went on to say that their financial analysts had apparently determined that they could save at least half the actual loss if they could get property owners to take a quick check and sign off on their claim.

Based upon what we were experiencing, their plan was pretty obvious; if they waited us out they figured that sooner or later we'd cave like so many others were doing and take a check. We didn't!

Instead, we gave them an ultimatum, come up with a reasonable settlement or we would start to make repairs without them. They didn't, so we began using our own money to gut the house and prepare it for reconstruction.

We had a large POD, one of those "store it" boxes, dropped on our driveway and, along with our builder, began salvaging items we felt could be saved.

Having just finished remodeling prior to Charley's arrival, there were several items we didn't want to see end up in a dumpster.

By the time our initial effort was completed we were down to four outer walls, the trusses, and studs.

As if looking at that wasn't enough to cause a mental breakdown, mold was beginning to move across the rafters. It had to be stopped before it spread through the entire rafter structure and down the inside of the outer walls.

After months of fighting with insurance adjusters, our patience had run out. We'd filed with the state and were notified that the insurance company would have to meet us in state sponsored mediation. After much hemming and hawing and with help from the state and our builder, our insurer was forced to cough up a reasonable amount of money to rebuild the house according to the latest building codes as specified in our coverage.

They grudgingly agreed that as no one could tell what material prices were going to be like from day to day, they would step up, again within the terms of our coverage, and make good on our policy limits if we exceeded the negotiated estimate of costs.

As it turned out, even with a written agreement our insurance adjusters fought us every step of the way. We had to fight for every dime.

Promises, promises!

Promises, Promises

After ten days of waiting for insurance people that failed to show up most of the time, I told Carla there was no way we could continue to live like a family of drowned rats.

With roads open to traffic, the three of us drove to Venice, about forty-five miles north, to meet with a rental agent my sister had found. It was time to rent a house.

Having just come from a major disaster you would think rental people would show some sympathy. I guess when they know they suddenly have more business than they have houses to rent, and you tell them you have three cats, and they see that you have a German shepherd, they cringe.

One of the realtors my sister had found was more than willing to show us a house. However, the house he showed us looked like a double wide trailer out of the 1930s. It was pathetic, and the property surrounding it looked even worse.

I took the agent aside and told him I didn't care what it cost or how big the security deposit for damage, I wanted a real house and to quit screwing us around.

Shazzam! His cash register jingled. He had a beautiful home in a new gated community on Venice Island, backing up to the Intracoastal waterway. However, he didn't know what the owners would say upon learning that the renting family had cats and a large dog.

"Well," I said, "I guess we'll never know until you call. And when you do, tell them to name their security deposit and that I promise to leave their house in better shape than we find it." That was a promise he could put in writing!

We drove back to his office and waited while he tried to reach the owner.

While we waited Sabrina went to work on all of the agents. Before you could say, "Sit. Stay," she had them all fawning over her, and who could resist? With one leg in a cast, she was irresistible.

The owner of the house was in a board meeting and his assistant promised that he would call when his meeting ended. A couple of hours later we signed a lease for a year. Now all we had to do was find a mover. Good luck.

When we finally found one and were able to enter our new rental house for the first time, we were surprised that Sabrina seemed to be taking the move quite well. Maybe after all she'd been through she knew that this was only temporary.

Wondering about the cats? No problem. Anyplace we put their litter box was home!

Once we learned that we only had twelve months of rental coverage and having lost nearly two weeks waiting for insurance adjusters and nearly four months before reaching a settlement, we began to push forward in earnest. What were the insurance adjusters doing as our rental coverage time slipped away? Well, they did their best to move even slower.

Shortly after Charley passed, I found myself visiting with our neighbors at the end of our canal, Ron and Sue. Their house was damaged, so they were living in their bus-type motor home. Thanks to the power the motor home generated, they were able to run their appliances inside their house while at the same time providing power for appliances and air conditioning inside the motor home.

I'd stopped by to see how they were doing, and when they heard we expected to lose quite a bit of frozen food when we moved, they offered us storage space in a freezer they kept in the garage.

While we were talking, their builder stopped by to see if they needed any help.

When they were through talking, I asked their builder if he'd be willing to help us, as we had no idea who built our home.

Jim said he'd take a look and, after seeing what was left of our house, agreed to rebuild it.

Now I know what you're thinking. "Of course he'd offer to help. Look at the money he'd make."

Nothing could have been further from the truth. Jim was one of the few builders on the Isles that went out of his way trying to get with every person he'd ever worked for to see if they needed help. In this instance, looking for work was a no-brainer; all you had to do was look around.

As it turned out, Jim's heart was bigger than his capability. He took on more work than he should have. However, over the two years it took to fight with the insurance company during the rebuilding process, he never failed to make himself available for meetings, no matter how he was pressed for time.

Looking back, I don't know if we would have made it without Jim. When you step back and look at what you are facing after a hurricane, I'm sure many people declare, "I give up, or we are out of here!"

Four months of fighting and our own efforts and money had taken our house to a point where we could begin to think about rebuilding — all of it done without assurance the insurance company would honor our policy.

We weren't holding out for any special favors or more help than our coverage allowed. All we wanted to do was to bring our house back to what it was before Charley, only stronger, as called for by the new codes and our policy.

No matter what the insurance company had agreed to provide, their word meant nothing.

Because the damage to our house exceeded 50 percent of the structure, the policy stated that the insurer could demand that it be demolished and a new one built in its place.

Deciding whether to allow us to rebuild as we wanted or scrap the house and start all over provided our insurer with a golden opportunity to drag their feet.

Meanwhile our rental coverage clock kept ticking. With less than eight months of rental coverage remaining, a mortgage to pay and a house that needed to be rebuilt — you do the math!

Once we exited mediation, Jim moved quickly to begin work on our house.

Before reconstruction could start, he had to address our ever expanding mold problem. Nothing could be done in the house until Jim finished cleaning it up and a state licensed inspector certified in writing that he could begin construction.

All of the plumbing and electrical wiring had to be ripped out and replaced with materials that met the latest building code — this took its toll on time.

The rental coverage that remained went by before we knew it. Our home in the Isles was now closed in but only partially finished. We still lacked water, cabinets in the kitchen and baths, light fixtures, plumbing fixtures, and air conditioning.

Jim had done his best not to let us down. Knowing when our rental coverage ended, he told us to move back at the end of twelve months, promising to make the house livable as quickly as possible.

We crossed our fingers and moved back after thirteen months rather than continuing to make both rental and mortgage payments.

And what about our rental house in Venice?

During our stay we evacuated to Orlando with Sabrina and the cats to wait out the outer edges of hurricane Frances.

When Jeanne came ashore, we stayed and did the best we could to wind-proof and protect the house. This included going out in sixty-mile-an-hour winds and rain to save two of the owner's palm trees. We tied one off to a telephone pole and the other to a more substantial tree.

Prior to each storm, we did everything in our power to see that the house was protected. We'd told the owners we would treat their property as if it was our own — and that's what we did!

Evacuation isn't an exact science. During one of our evacuations we drove to Troy, Alabama, to avoid a hurricane that was expected to come up the west coast of Florida.

We'd stayed at the Holiday Inn Express in Troy several times when we were making trips back and forth to our new home with items we didn't want to trust to the movers. This particular Holiday Inn was pet friendly, so we knew we wouldn't be turned away.

When we arrived and checked in, the parking lot looked as though we were back in Florida. Nearly every license plate was from Florida. Apparently everyone else knew about this pet friendly escape. Cats, dogs, birds, you name it; they were all in temporary residence.

Talk about meeting and making new friends. Sabrina seemed to find them wherever she went, and this short stay was no exception.

Sometimes your best laid plans run amuck. On our first night, we turned on the Weather Channel and damned if the hurricane hadn't changed course.

Originally, it was expected to travel up the west coast of Florida and then turn east, inland, and move up the Atlantic side.

Surprise! The latest course had Wilma heading for the Pensacola, Florida area, then turning north on a line that would take it straight to Troy.

We stayed in Troy only until Wilma had declared her intentions. When we saw that her track was going to take her farther west and then north, a mass exodus of the Holiday Inn began. The Florida contingent packed their bags and headed for the east coast of Florida and a slow return home before Wilma came ashore.

Sabrina was beginning to see evacuations as a treat. She may not have known why she was being evacuated, but as long as she was going for a long ride in the car with us, and her bowls and toys were packed, she was a happy child.

It's been said that you can run, but you can't hide. Based upon our experience in Troy, maybe there's some truth to that!

Because of our concern for the Venice house, we became friends with the owners. During our stay, they visited with us on three occasions.

Carla and I had gone through the house carefully prior to our furniture arriving. We identified several problems that prior renters hadn't mentioned and the real estate people had missed. Once the owners went over our list, they asked if we would allow workmen to come in and repair or replace anything that needed work. We told them to "send them in and we would be happy to make sure the repairs were done right."

As promised, we left their house in better shape than we found it. I guess that's why, knowing that we'd be moving back to Punta Gorda once our one year lease was up, the owners told us to take as much additional time as we needed if our house wasn't ready. They said not to worry about a new lease, we could rent month-to-month if we needed more time. As it turned out, we did stay almost a month, but finally, ready or not, we wanted to get back home.

When we turned in the keys to the Venice house it not only passed inspection, we got back our entire pet deposit.

Oh, in case I failed to elaborate, six months before Charley wreaked havoc upon our house, we had remodeled both bathrooms, put granite counter tops in the kitchen and had an interior decorator come to help us choose colors for a complete interior/exterior repaint. So much time, effort, work, and expense, all destroyed in a matter of hours.

Little by little, and what seemed inch by inch, our house slowly became a home again. Finally, twenty-two months after Charley hit, we celebrated the erection of a new pool cage. The rebuilding process was finally finished!

During that time we faced off with thirteen insurance adjusters. One would play "good cop" and work with us, the next was "the bad cop" threatening to hold up funds while he did his best to drive us nuts.

We never gave in to them, although at times we came very close.

A good friend of mine in Dallas, John Hart, came to our rescue shortly after Charley's visit. John just happens to be a lawyer with a very big international practice specializing in major industrial disasters. He called a principal in one of the adjustment investigation firms he worked with, and before we knew it, we had a professional from one of the world's largest firms working for us pro bono.

Neither David Hahn or his firm would accept a penny from us, yet David oversaw every move we made every step of the way. He was outstanding.

Throughout the rebuilding of our house David stayed in the background, helping us to write appropriate letters and directing our every move at meetings with the insurance company and their adjusters.

David happened to be a big dog lover so, as you can imagine, he and our girl got along famously.

He and his group were in the process of overseeing the rebuild of more than four hundred condos that had been destroyed or badly damaged by Charley. Yet with more than enough work on his plate, he never failed to make time to talk to or be with us when we needed him.

When we reached those points when we were sure we couldn't take it anymore, and there were several such instances, David would talk with us, settle us down, refocus us, and have us up and marching forward before we knew it!

As for Sabrina, she made lots of new friends while she was on her extended vacation on Venice Island. As usual, she stole the hearts of the people she met. The more people loved on her, the more her stomach seemed to remain settled.

The one thing I think she missed was my not leaving every Friday morning for our neighborhood men's breakfast. It was her time to demonstrate a level of love that knew no boundaries – when I left and upon my return home.

Every Friday she would rush to the door as I headed out, positioning her body so that I couldn't ignore her. I would bend down, rub her head, massage her ears and promise to come back soon. Next, I would be lavished with licks and cries as I went out the door. She would remain at the door until I returned.

If leaving was an event, returning was all the more raucous. I'd open the door and be greeted by seventy-five pounds of German shepherd trying to jump into my arms. When she wasn't trying to reach my face for a lick, she'd be crying, spinning around and anxiously waiting for me to get down on my knees so I could rub her belly. If someone was watching the two of us, they probably would have thought I'd been gone for a year rather than a couple of hours. What a welcome each and every time I came home. More often than not, after hugging and rubbing on her, I would thank God once again for having loaned her to me.

During reconstruction the three of us made the trip from Venice to our home in Punta Gorda Isles on a daily basis. Some days, because of the times set for meetings, we found ourselves making two and three trips in a day.

We logged close to twenty thousand miles meeting with sub-contractors, our builder, FEMA, the SBA, and our insurance company.

Our insurance company provided insurance coverage for our house, cars, and an overall umbrella policy. They knew why we were driving so much, and even so, they raised our automobile premium. That's right. We'd driven more miles than we had promised. The fact that we had a house to rebuild was obviously of no concern to them; they wanted their extra hundred bucks!

When the time came to move back to our home, you should have seen Sabrina; she was like a kid in a toy store as she ran back and forth in the house. All of her friends were there to greet her. She didn't know who to greet or allow too rub her belly-first. She was home at last and whether her house was finished or not, she was a very happy child!

Why am I spending so much time telling you about a hurricane and the people that came into our lives? Because it was a moment in time that took the three of us, and many of our friends beyond the breaking point as we surveyed the wreckage of our home and lives. It was a time when we gave thanks for having good friends, and most importantly that all of us came through Charley without a scratch.

We cried together, worked together, hugged and consoled each other. We even had a few laughs together. God seems to find a way to make even the worst of times tolerable.

Sabrina's world revolved around a single thought, a place for everything and everything in its place. Suddenly, she'd been displaced. Yet all we had to do is look at her, to see how lucky we were.

Before Charley, her last visit to the grass at night included an inspection of the neighborhood. She knew where every car was parked. If she observed the slightest change, or heard a strange sound, her tail would go down. I'd feel her pressing her body against my hip — prepared to protect me.

Immediately after Charley there was no telling what went through her mind. Her surroundings had changed — drastically!

It was a time when we felt sure that if anything was going to tip the scales where her health was concerned, seeing her surroundings in shambles would do it. If that didn't do it, having to move to a strange new place, even though it was just an hour away, would normally guarantee a physical reaction.

Thanks to medications and a lot of loving she made it, we made it, and all of our displaced friends finally returned home.

Sabrina had come though a major disaster with flying colors.

Maybe she did because God was watching over her. She had been through so much that maybe this time, was her time to shine!

It took a while for everything in the neighborhood to return to its proper place.

However, she was always by our side, ready to protect us, even if she might not know why.

Given half a chance, Sabrina would have gone into our house in the middle of the hurricane, cast and all, to find out who was responsible for the carnage that was taking place.

As our house became more livable, David Hahn joined us for a home-cooked meal. For the better part of two years he'd either been cooking for himself or eating in restaurants.

He was also our guest for a going away dinner at his favorite restaurant as his work in the area was nearing completion.

During this time, I became more convinced than ever that love is a two-way street. It doesn't always come in the form of licks and tail wags. Sometimes it's just a look. Other times: an action, a fierce growl as a sign of protection, or a neighbor stopping what he's doing to offer a helping hand. Sabrina and our neighbors were always there for us, just as we tried to be there for them.

Where our pets are concerned, who knows when or how the bond between us is formed. Having had the good fortune to live it, I've got to believe it comes from the heart and that it's unconditional!

For nearly eleven years, no matter how she was feeling, Sabrina's love of people never faltered. No matter where she was or who she was with, the love she dispensed day in and day out never stopped.

As for me, I found myself working overtime to return that love, and I wouldn't trade a minute.

Unbeknown to us, while Sabrina was now bounding around like the puppy she had always been, she was about to face a new challenge, one that we never saw coming. This time we weren't going to be able to do anything about it. Like it or not, it would prove what pet owners the world over have always known, God only loans us these fabulous creatures, and all good things must come to an end.

Goodbye, My Love. Have Good Doggy Dreams

I've often thought that life was just a stopover in time, a trip from here to somewhere new.

The time we spend at each stop isn't guaranteed or contracted for in advance. Rather, it's one of life's little surprises.

Who we are, what we've accumulated, even our surroundings have been loaned to us for an unspecified time.

That was why I cherished my time with Sabrina. I knew that nothing in life lasts forever.

I repeatedly told her that she couldn't move on before me. Each time, she would cock her head, look at me, and listen as if she knew exactly what I was saying as she hung on my every word.

We were weeks away from her eleventh birthday and Christmas. Her new toys for each celebration had been purchased and hidden away. I remember telling Carla how lucky we'd been to have had Sabrina for so long considering everything she'd been through.

Sabrina's body had faced more medical challenges than anybody should have to endure. Yet each time she seemed to bounce back a happier and more lovable puppy than before.

She was blessed with a love of life and people that rubbed off on you. You might enter our house with a frown on your face, but if she wasn't taking a nap in her kennel — you left smiling. When she was near, I found myself seeing, feeling, and enjoying my time and surroundings all the more.

Because of her health and physical problems, we treated each day, month, and year she was with us as a gift, knowing all the while that her medical problems could take her from us at any time.

We'd been told that German shepherds lived an average of seven to eight years, so you can see why we considered ourselves to be very lucky.

Sabrina surprised us and amazed the vets that took such great care to keep her healthy.

Who says lots of love and spoiling a child rotten doesn't work?

Suddenly we noticed she was off her feed. She was never a great eater unless we gave her a bowl of veggies, but this latest lack of interest in food, even for her, seemed excessive.

Then one night, she began making guttural sounds while trying to vomit.

As I recall, the first in a series of these episodes began on a weekend. Carla had just taken Sabrina out to do her business before bedtime on Sunday. When she was through and ready to come inside she was so weak it took all of her willpower just to make it to the front door.

Carla called to me from outside and together we coaxed Sabrina inside and into her crate in our bedroom. Each step was an effort. Once she was settled in, Carla noticed that her gums were pale, not the deep pink they should have been.

"I don't like the looks of this," she said, "I think we need to get her to Dr. Bivens first thing in the morning." That was all I needed to hear. As in the past, if she saw something she didn't like, she was usually right.

Dr. Bivens saw Sabrina first thing Monday morning. She listened to us describe what had happened over the weekend, then ran a series of blood tests that all came up negative.

Carla mentioned Sabrina's total lack of interest in food. This was nothing new. Once again, for reasons I don't remember, Dr. Bivens said she suspected a problem with Sabrina's pancreas and suggested we take her up to see Dr. Ward in Sarasota immediately for an ultrasound and additional tests.

Dr. Heidi Ward had been Sabrina's internist throughout most of her eleven years. She also happened to be an oncologist.

We called ahead and as then drove to her Sarasota office. It was a very quiet ride. Worried, we waited impatiently until the receptionist called Sabrina's name. The three of us were placed in an examining room where, as we waited for Dr. Ward, I spent most of the time, petting and talking to Sabrina. This didn't stop when she was placed on the examining table. As she lay quietly, I had one hand under her head and the other was gently rubbing her ears.

Dr. Ward completed her initial exam then she and her assistant took Sabrina to another room and, while we waited, conducted an ultrasound and additional X-rays.

When she returned, she showed us the film and discussed the ultrasound. The results weren't good. She told us that Sabrina was bleeding internally. Although blood was masking most of the area in question, her liver, she could see a tumor, a potentially large one, but at the moment, most of it was being hidden by the bleeding.

Was she in pain? You wouldn't know it to look at my little girl. Time and again, I was in awe of her serenity. Throughout her life we never knew when she was in pain. As far as my brave little girl was concerned, today was just another day — albeit at a doctor's office.

During nearly eleven years with us, Sabrina never once treated her doctors aggressively. As long as I was standing next to her, stroking her head, she would lie quietly on their examining table and let them do their work. I would bend over and give her an occasional kiss on the head, whispering softly that everything was going to be all right and that I wouldn't let anyone hurt her. When I was near, any sign of agitation seemed to disappear.

We listened as Dr. Ward explained that even though blood was masking the extent of the tumor in her liver, she didn't think Sabrina's aging body could tolerate surgery.

I asked Dr. Ward about chemotherapy and radiation, and she said that at Sabrina's age she would have difficulty tolerating the treatment. She explained that it might add a few very uncomfortable months to Sabrina's life, but she wouldn't recommend it.

Instead, she suggested that as Sabrina didn't appear to be in pain, we take her home and wait for her to have one last life-taking episode. However, she pointed out that if it happened while we were out of the house we might very well come home and find that she had passed.

I told her that neither option was acceptable. I had no intention of allowing my little girl to live her remaining months in pain or leave without my being there to tell her how much I loved her.

I had made repeated promises to God and I intended to keep them!

Knowing how much faith we had in Dr. Oakes, she suggested we take Sabrina up to Largo for a second opinion. Dr. Ward felt that he might be better able to gauge the potential for a miracle, the result of surgery.

I will never forget that afternoon. As I stood waiting to pay Dr. Ward's bill, she came out of an examining room, put her arms around me, gave me a hug, and we both cried.

She knew how much Sabrina meant to me, probably as much or more than anyone. She'd treated her through anxiety and stomach attacks from the time we moved to Florida.

This was a lady that lived with the death of pets on a regular basis. You would think that it would have hardened her, but it didn't. From that day she was more than a vet — she was a trusted friend.

We called the surgical center as we drove home and made an appointment to return once again to Largo.

The next morning found us waiting in the lobby for Dr. Oakes. Having spoken to Dr. Ward, he knew why we were coming and what to expect.

We always knew when he was coming down the hall. Even before we saw him, we heard his familiar shout, "hey you!" This had been his customary greeting to our little girl during all the years we had known him. The minute Sabrina heard his voice, she would go into hiding and today was no exception.

The morning consisted of more scans, another ultrasound, and then the words we knew were coming but had refused to accept. There would be no miracle today.

"Dr. Ward's assessment was right. In fact, now that more of the blood that was masking her organs has cleared away and we can get a clearer picture of Sabrina's body, her liver is laced with tumors.

"I can operate, but I don't recommend it. I don't think I can get at all of the tumors. Even if Sabrina came through surgery she'd need chemo and radiation therapy to get at any remaining tumors. The surgery and those treatments wouldn't be kind to her, and at best they might buy her three months."

There was that number again!

We sat in stunned silence. Chemo and surgery, two options with the same end result, having to stand by and watch my little girl's life being peeled away, a layer at a time.

Maybe she'd be with me for three months, but how could I be so thoughtless? I'd watched friends fight for their lives and lose to cancer — watched as their bodies were destroyed by long-shot cures that failed. I would not sentence my little girl to a three month living hell.

I couldn't imagine my beautiful little girl being slowly, painfully reduced to skin and bones just so that I might spend a few extra days with her.

Carla and I sat in silence for a few minutes just thinking and crying. Matt Oakes broke the silence.

"If it were me, I would take her home, keep her as comfortable as possible, and allow the tumors to run their course."

Watching our reaction, he offered a second solution, "I could put Sabrina to sleep." We declined. I'm sure he knew we would. This wasn't the time or the place to make a decision like that.

We thanked him for always being there when we needed him, stood, and shook hands.

As we started to leave, Matt bent down and gave Sabrina a big hug and asked us to keep him advised of our decision.

I knew the decision that needed to be made. I had promised myself, and more importantly I had promised God, that I would never allow Sabrina to live in pain needlessly. I knew I couldn't go back on that promise no matter how difficult it was going to be to keep.

Sabrina had lived with pain for so many years. Endured surgery upon surgery, with never so much as a whimper. As tears rolled down my cheek, it was obvious that my little girl was far braver than her father.

When my left knee was replaced with artificial parts and I went through months of rehab, there were times when I thought I wanted to die. I swore I would never allow my one good leg to be put through that torture.

Yet rehab after rehab, Sabrina marched forward with a smile on her face. She may have been hurting, I'm sure she was, but you would never know it to look at her. If anything, we had to hold her down in order to keep her from overdoing it.

She had been through so much since the day she was born. Yet from that very first day that I held her in my arms, she asked so little and had always given more love than she received.

In return for our love and care, Sabrina had given us nearly eleven years of a joy we never knew existed. After all, a dog in our lives — who'd a thunk it!

As I began the drive home from Largo, I found myself recounting the years, the surgeries, and the joy she had brought into our lives. Try as I might, the tears kept coming.

I pulled off on the side of the road and asked Carla to drive. Not long after she took over the wheel, we were both crying. I don't remember how many times we changed places, much less, how we managed to get home without causing an accident as all the while, Sabrina slept peacefully on her back seat of "her" car — without a care in the world.

While Carla was driving I kept reaching back between the seats to stroke my little girl. Every so often I would stop and whisper to her, but she was sound asleep. Just as I told her each night before going to sleep, she was dreaming I'm sure, "of angels." From time to time, I allowed my hand to remain on her still body and as I relaxed it, suddenly, she would begin licking my hand. I believe this was her way of telling me not to worry. I will always remember this response as one born of love.

I couldn't stop reaching back. Maybe this was my way of telling God that I wasn't ready to release her — as if I had a choice.

Maybe I just wanted to know that she was still with us — still in her favorite spot when traveling. After all, as far as she was concerned, she was going for a ride with her parent's and she was right where she belonged.

As long as I could feel her body moving as she breathed, I knew that she still belonged to me!

By the time we arrived home I knew what had to be done. I would keep my promise and do what was right for our biggest, little girl.

I knew I wasn't the first person to experience the loss of a special friend, and I certainly wouldn't be the last. However, during that drive home I came to appreciate what those that had come before me must have experienced. All of us had been blessed to find so much love, and in the end feel so much pain.

I know some of you are thinking, "If it was me, I'd want my child with me as long as possible." Sure, we could have allowed Dr. Oakes to remove a good portion of Sabrina's liver and God only knows what else. Or we could have done nothing, kept her with us and watched as her life slowly slipped away.

I thought about those options, but only for a moment.

I wanted my brave little girl to return to God the way he had loaned her to me, with that ever-present smile on her face. That's the way I would always remember her.

That night Sabrina enjoyed all of her favorite treats.

Carla and I reminisced about all the good years we'd had. How blessed we had been to have this four-legged miracle come into our lives in such a strange way. We had never wanted a dog — never expected to own one. And yet, here she was. No one thought she would be with us for so long. Nearly eleven years. Where had the days gone? I guess because she filled our house with so much love and laughter, we didn't notice the time passing us by.

Cats were always running around in our house. Now, we were down to two. Our house was no longer filled with four-legged children. It was nearly as empty as our hearts. I was sixty-nine a little late to be starting with a dog all over again. Carla was ten years younger, but had said so many times that when the "children" were gone, she didn't want any more, and I believed her.

We'd experienced the loss of several cats over the years and shed more than a few tears.

Then suddenly, God delivered a stranger to our door, and it was as if having a dog was meant to be.

One thing I knew for certain, after nearly eleven years with Sabrina, nothing could replace the joys, the heartache, and the love that we experienced during our trip through time together — absolutely nothing!

I sat on the floor with Sabrina that night, after the long ride home from Largo, and we talked and talked. Well, we didn't actually talk. As always she listened while I tried to explain what somehow I think she already knew.

She had been loaned to us, and it was now time for her to return to a pain free place. That, in and of itself, should have consoled Carla and I, but it didn't!

My little girl loved squeaky balls. Carla had already picked up one to wrap and place under the Christmas tree in a few weeks. It was a red and blue football with little green and red prongs to stimulate her gums. Christmas would come early this year for Sabrina — we gave her the ball that evening.

New toys were always greeted with enthusiasm, and her football was no exception. I tossed it to her, and she was off and running through the house as if there was nothing wrong with her. She may have been weak, but she pranced around that night, squeaking the ball, showing it to us and squealing with joy. That's how I wanted to remember her — a puppy forever!

If she could have talked to us at that moment I'm sure she would have exclaimed, *"Sick, who's sick? Not me!"*

For years, Sabrina always slept on the floor beside me. This evening, when Carla and I called it a night, there she was, half asleep but waiting for her hug and kiss, and my nightly command to "Have good doggy dreams and dream of angels."

Something else was waiting for me. She had taken her new red ball and placed it on the floor at the head of the bed where I couldn't miss it. It was as if she was saying, *"Please take care of this for me."*

We'd already made an appointment with Dr. Bivens for the next day. There was no sense in waiting, the longer we did, the harder the task ahead of us would become. We asked to be her last appointment of the day, and it came far too quickly.

We wanted to come in late, after her regular patients so that we wouldn't see or be seen by any of them. We wanted to be alone with our little girl. Dr. Bivens understood.

As we talked with her that afternoon, she explained what was going to take place.

Although we'd been through the procedure with our cats, we chose not to interrupt her.

Sabrina would receive three shots. The first two would calm and begin to place her at rest. The final shot would send her back to a God that I knew was waiting her arrival.

I sat down on the floor in the examining room. Sabrina lay down across my legs and placed her head in my lap. I bent over and began hugging her. With each injection I whispered in her ear, "Don't worry. Soon you'll be home." In between sobs, I told her how much I loved her and how much we would miss her. Most importantly, I told her that she would always be with us.

I sat on the floor and just cried. At that moment, I'd have given anything for just a few more days with her. I had promised that she would never be allowed to be in pain needlessly, and I intended to keep that promise to her and to God for having allowed me to keep her for so long.

I could feel a difference as each needle entered her body. With the first two her body gradually began to relax in my arms.

Then it was time for the third shot, and suddenly she was gone forever. She looked so beautiful as she lay with her head in my lap. She was still — perfectly at ease. I wrapped my arms around her, pulled her head and shoulders to my chest, and hung on to her tightly, willing her to wake up, and I continued to cry as the pain of her loss enveloped me.

This child of God had come into my life by accident. She had stolen my heart, and now she had broken it. Along the way she had taught me the meaning of unconditional love

Sabrina left my world the way she had come into my life, in my arms!

She was gone, but somehow I knew we would always be together.

We'd made arrangements with Dr. Bivens to have Sabrina cremated. I wanted my little girl with me when it was my time to go, and this was one way to make sure that when that day came, we would be together again, just as I had promised.

We picked up her ashes a few days later. I transferred them from the tin box they had come in, into a beautiful German shepherd cookie jar that had held many of her treats. Then, I placed the jar, pictures, and remembrances of her on shelves in my office so that I could visit with her while I worked or just spent time at the computer.

Christmas just wasn't the same. Sabrina wasn't sitting on the floor beside us patiently waiting our command to go find the present that was always wrapped and hidden under the tree waiting for her.

Once released, somehow she always knew exactly which present was hers. Once found, she'd make repeated attempts to unwrap it. When she determined it was impossible, she would walk over to me and drop it in my lap. She knew that I would stop what I was doing and unwrap it for her.

Carla and I celebrated our twenty-fifth anniversary two months after Sabrina left us. It was our silver anniversary, and neither of us had a clue what to get each other.

As a matter a fact, neither of us cared much for silver.

Then Carla came across a company that made silver and gold pet cremation jewelry. One of their offerings was a silver dog bone that could hold a small amount of ashes. The bone could be carried on our key chain or worn around our neck as a pendant. We ordered two as gifts to each other and when they arrived, carefully funneled some of Sabrina's ashes into each one.

She may have been gone, but as I promised, she is never far away. I carry that little silver bone along with her red, heart-shaped dog tag, on my key chain.

For nearly eleven years I could always count on her to be at my side, and now I knew she would be there forever!

There was a time when I was sure that nothing in life was free. Now I know that I was wrong! When we bought Sabrina, I thought two hundred and fifty dollars was a lot to pay for a pup. That purchase turned out to be the best investment Carla and I ever made.

How could I place a price tag on watching her graduate from her first puppy school?

Seeing her joy as she stuck her nose into a cold, heaping bowl of vanilla ice cream?

Watching her as she launched her long body into the air as she attempted to fly from one end of our house in Tennessee to the other?

Attaining "oneness" with her at boot camp?

Seeing the love she shared with everyone, including a pig named Dandelion and a Labrador retriever named Tucker?

Watching her cry out with joy and prance around squeaking a new toy?

Sitting in the closet with Carla and I as hurricane Charley tore our house apart? Even with one leg in a cast, she was ready to react as all German shepherds are created to do — protect us from anyone that tried to harm us.

The list of memories is endless!

Say what you will, but I believe that God has a hand in placing every one of his special gifts and he chose to place Sabrina with me.

He loans these wonderful creations to us, and when he asks that they be returned, he leaves us blessed with so many wonderful stories to share.

Will Rogers knew what he was talking about when he said, "If there aren't any dogs in heaven, then I want to go wherever they were."

Over the past few years, Carla and I have watched a number of dog trainers come and go on television. Most, if not all of them, made it perfectly clear to viewers and especially those watching that owned dogs, that they were just that — dogs — and should be treated as such.

They pointed out the importance of drawing lines that defined the limitations and expectations owners needed to establish if they were to become pack leaders for their pet.

I couldn't agree more — or less.

Sabrina knew the difference between right and wrong: not eating the furniture and jumping up to greet visitors.

She also knew that twenty-four hours a day, three hundred and sixty-five days of every year she was loved and that we cared deeply about her.

In return, she lavished us with love. No questions asked. No demands made. Her every waking hour was spent finding new ways to bring a smile to our faces.

Time and again, friends asked us why we kept spending money on Sabrina for veterinarians, specialists, and surgery. They couldn't understand why we were willing to place our lives on hold in order to see to her needs and have her with us.

In eleven years we'd driven thousands of miles and spent thousands of dollars in order to keep Sabrina by our side, and I wouldn't have had it any other way.

Fail to do whatever was necessary — right now?

Out of the question!

Give up on my little girl and just put her down?

Not until I knew it was absolutely necessary!

Will Rogers was a man after my own heart. When it's my time to go, I hope I'll have an opportunity to meet him. I'm sure we'll have plenty of stories to swap. After all, what would heaven be like without our pets, tails wagging, waiting to guide us when we arrive?

As I look back on my time with Sabrina, I'd have to say that when God made her he included a happy gene that guaranteed she would dispense love and affection 'round the clock no matter what her physical condition might be.

If given the opportunity to raise her again would I treat her differently? Would I want to change anything? Never! I believe God had a reason for sending Lokey to our door on a cold winter day. He knew that we would not turn him away.

When we found a new home for him, I believe he knew that we would find, as so many have, that we needed a dog in our lives, and he had just the right one waiting for us!

Sabrina may have been treated as more than a dog by Carla and me. I'm sure that most trainers would have been appalled by our behavior, but as far as we were concerned, she was, and always will be, our biggest little girl.

Sabrina's gone and yet it's as if she never left me. Often after I've fallen asleep, I find myself returning to October 27, 2006. I'm holding her head in my arms, watching as that last needle enters her body, and I am crying.

Other times, I imagine the two of us running together. Our legs are strong, and as we run Sabrina looks up at me with that ever-present smile on her face. It's as if she is trying to soften the loss we share. "*Don't worry, Dad. We'll be together again. I promise.*"

I stop to catch my breath, and she continues to run, disappearing over the horizon. It's as if I've been running in an effort to push back the clock, to erase the memory of the day she was called to return home.

Carla and I realize she's gone. Yet that doesn't stop us from talking about her or accidentally calling our new little girl by the wrong name every now and again. I can only hope that Tia understands.

That's right, although we both said "absolutely, positively never again," where another dog was concerned, we were wrong, but you will need to read on to find out more about our new little girl.

I think God entrusted me with a new little girl because he knew that I needed another child to love and that I would take good care of her, just as I had before, no matter what, until it is once again time for her to return home.

Sabrina lived life to the fullest without fail every day. She taught me that words are meaningless without actions — that *love* is just a word unless it is unconditional and that life is a gift.

Through her, I learned that life isn't always fair. Sabrina lived with pain throughout most of her life although she never showed it. As for me — I didn't handle her pain very well. There were times when I found myself asking and sometimes demanding that God explain to me, why he was treating my little girl "so harshly?"

Although I have no way of proving it, I believe he was testing the limits of my resolve. After all, he loaned one of his children to me and needed to know how I would respond when "the chips were down." Would I give her away, put her to sleep, or would I be there for her, no matter what?

Did I have the strength of character he believed that I possessed when he entrusted Sabrina to me?

No matter how many obstacles life threw at my little girl, she shook them off and as she did, my love for her grew stronger. When she was recovering from surgery I found myself reaching in to the deepest corners of my soul to comfort her.

Through prayer I discovered an inner strength and commitment that equaled Sabrina's courage.

Make no mistake, I was not the brave one in this relationship, Sabrina was. Her determination and will to overcome made me a better person!

Carla and I have made our burial plans. One day, we will be united with several pet children as our ashes and those of Sabrina and five of our cats are released into the ocean — completing our circle of life.

Wondering what happened to Sabrina's little red football? It's in my nightstand drawer and will remain there until I return it to her myself — just as I promised!

Tia the Terrible

Several times during my nearly eleven years with Sabrina, I told Carla that I would never, ever bring another dog in to our home. Sabrina was my first, and when she was returned home I didn't think I could handle the emotional pain that I knew I would have to face a second time.

I'd watched neighbors and relatives, upon losing a pet. At first, I didn't understand their pain — I do now!

Maybe it was because Sabrina's life had been one of constant pain as she traveled from one major surgery to the next. Each time, I relived her past surgeries as I waited for word from her surgeons and each time I could feel a piece of my heart being cut away.

Time and again, I thanked God for allowing her to return to me after each operation, but our years together took their toll on my state of mind.

In my heart I knew, or at least I thought I did, that bringing another dog in to my life would simply repeat the emotional pain I felt when it was time for me to give her back to God. Just the thought of another four-legged child being taken away from me was enough to persuade me that one child was enough.

Our first night without her in the house changed both of our minds. There was emptiness, a silence. The toys had stopped squeaking. The laughter had stopped. Carla and I were never alone when Sabrina was with us, and now the two of us knew that something was missing!

Even during those times when Sabrina was curled up on the floor next to me sleeping, Carla and I found ourselves talking to or about our little girl.

She brought something special into our home and our lives — a spontaneous eruption of love and merriment.

It didn't take long for both of us to conclude that we needed another puppy. I think we knew it within the first twenty-four hours of her passing, but it took us a couple of months to make a decision.

I don't think Carla wanted to broach the subject. She could see what the loss of Sabrina was doing to me. I could be walking around the house, or sitting down reading and all of a sudden I would start thinking about her and I would break into tears.

Frankly, neither of us seemed to know what to do. Did we want another dog, and if so, did we want another large dog? That resulted in the question — did we want another German shepherd?

If that was our choice, would a new female pup constantly remind us of Sabrina and lessen our love for the new child?

We had more questions than we had answers, so we decided to bring an impartial third party into our decision making process — but who, and where would we find him?

If you find yourself in a similar state of mind after losing a special friend, know that there are people waiting to help you understand that you are not alone. These people can help you to move through the grieving process and beyond. That's right, I said grieving process, because that is exactly what is happening to you — you are grieving.

Most of these people are specially trained and willing to spend as much time as it takes to help you understand why you feel as you do about your loss.

After doing some research on the internet we decided to call the Iams Grief Counseling Center.

If you are a pet owner, or more specifically, a breeder, as we had been for so many years, we felt we could trust the Iams name. As it turned out, we were right!

We called and were transferred to Mitch. He represented Iams quite well. His time with us was never an issue. He talked to us for over an hour the first time we called.

Mitch showed great patience, understanding and caring as Carla and I repeatedly broke into tears as we described our loss. When we were through talking he emphasized that we keep his name and call back whenever the pain of our loss was great or we just wanted to talk.

He was right about the pain and even more so about needing someone to talk with — we just didn't realize it when our first call ended.

Over the next several months we spoke with Mitch a number of times. He understood what we were going through, and because he'd experienced a loss of his own — he knew that our pain was not going to disappear overnight.

During one of our calls, and after talking with him for some time, I asked, "How do you do it? How do you listen to one stranger after another, day after day, all of us coming to you with our hearts on our sleeve?"

His answer was simple, "I love what I am doing, and like all of you, I lost a very special friend, so I know and appreciate what each of you that I talk with are feeling!"

Mitch repeatedly reminded us that the grief we were feeling would not disappear overnight.

During one of our last conversations, we told him we were thinking about another dog and had mixed feelings where bringing a new four-legged child in to the house was concerned. Unwilling to allow anything to get in our way, we expressed our desire to go out and buy another dog — immediately!

He listened, and slowly but surely, began to talk us out of making any snap decision. He reminded us that we needed time to reflect and to fully appreciate what we had lost, before bringing another four-legged child in to our house, and yes, he talked us out of our need to act — now!

Because of Sabrina's health and anxiety problems we hadn't vacationed without her in some time. We had dedicated our life to her needs and now, our life seemed to be spinning in empty circles.

Mitch had recommended that we "take our time," so, in a way, we did. Suddenly, we felt a need and desire to get out of the house and do some traveling — just the two of us, before committing to another puppy. We needed some alone time — together!

We had scheduled a trip to Detroit to visit our grandkids the end of April, so May, 2007, became our target date for finding a pup.

When we weren't traveling we agreed that we would begin searching for a top notch American German shepherd breeder. We knew that once we found a pup we'd have to once again, devote a year or more to training, loving, and acclimating our new child to her new family and surroundings.

Our first trip was an eight day cruise over New Year's. We celebrated our twenty-fifth anniversary on board as our anniversary date was January 1. Devious person that I am, I made plans in advance for a little surprise. Of course, I didn't bother to tell Carla — she would find out soon enough.

Once on board and in our cabin, we found an envelope with what appeared to be, a personal invitation from the Captain — or so Carla thought. We spiffed up a bit, and I took her up to what turned out to be the chapel, where we renewed our wedding vows.

The Royal Caribbean people did a beautiful job. There were white roses — Carla's favorite — champagne, and a photographer standing by to capture the moment, and several more, using several backdrops throughout the ship for his pictures. Needless to say, the most important love of my life was quite surprised. Of equal importance, I think the cruise afforded us an opportunity to place our thoughts of Sabrina and a new little girl on hold — and just concentrate on each other for a while.

For years we had wanted to see the Panama Canal, so shortly after we returned from the first cruise, we booked a second one and two months later, visited ruins in Mexico, the rivers of Costa Rica, and traveled the locks of the Canal. It was awesome!

When we weren't traveling, we did our homework relative to a new child. As you might guess, our minds were made up. We wanted another German shepherd. You've already heard me talk about them, so I'll try not to repeat myself. However, in my eyes they are four-legged art — the closest you can come to finding a human wrapped in fur.

During our nearly eleven years with Sabrina, we never stopped reading about the breed and breeders.

We watched every dog training show that came on television. Some, we agreed with, others, not so much.

This time, when we began our hunt for a puppy we were well "armed." I didn't head for the puppy classifieds in our local newspaper. I went straight to that information highway in the sky — the internet.

I found a website for the American German Shepherd Breeders Association of America and corresponded with several of their people. They were all very responsive and eager to talk with me.

Their president told me there would be a dog show in Ft. Myers, Florida, and gave me the date. He suggested it would be a great place to see the dogs perform and, most importantly, provide an opportunity to meet a number of breeders. We marked our calendar and planned to go.

He was right. The dogs showed off their ability to respond to their handlers, and we met and spoke with several breeders.

By the time the show was over we'd fallen in love with several dogs, and identified five breeders within three hundred miles of our home.

Prior to making our final decision to bring another German shepherd in to our life, I called Mitch one more time, I wanted his advice. I told him what we were planning to do and asked for his thoughts.

He knew my concerns before I explained them. If we purchased the same breed of dog, would I find myself always comparing her to Sabrina — thinking more about what I had lost then what I was gaining?

"When I lost my special child," Mitch explained, "I felt the same as you — never again. Then I realized how much I missed having a special friend around. I asked myself the same questions you're asking yourself now. Then I went out and bought another pup. The same breed as before.

"I've never regretted the decision. Matter a fact, before I knew it, I went out and bought a second one — a companion for the first!"

The best advice I can give you, "take your time and follow your hearts."

We did, although it wasn't long before we doubted our decision.

Shortly after the show, we began corresponding and talking with breeders on the phone regarding their plans for puppies.

We selected two breeders. However, as it turned out, we were only able to meet with one, as for one reason or another every time we tried to schedule a visit we had conflicting schedules.

We did visit Sue and Glenn Sherwood, of Glennwod Kennels. They'd been breeding and showing American German shepherds for many years and had a long list of show winners.

They had also been very active in the national and regional American German shepherd Breeders Association. We considered that a plus. Although they were 150 miles north of us, our trip to meet and explore turned out to be worth every mile.

Our visit began in their family room, with Glenn and Sue talking about, their breeding and puppy handling methods.

Next, they walked us through a picture gallery of their many show dogs. These were professional breeders and they were proud of every dog they had kept and trained to show, as well as being equally proud of the pups they had sold that had gone on to become big winners in the hands of new owners.

Make no mistake, there was nothing wrong with our first visit to breeders several years earlier — all, ran small kennels.

The Sherwood's had been in the business of breeding for competition for many years and as we listened to their history, there was no question — they knew their breed.

Once Glenn and Sue had answered all of our questions, they asked us if we would like to meet the parents of their next litter of puppies? As this group of pups would be available close to our target date, of course we said, "yes!"

We stood up, expecting to go out to their kennel building, and were asked to, "please sit down we'll bring mom and dad in to meet you."

The next thing we knew two absolutely beautiful and, most important, loveable shepherds came bounding in to the family room.

We didn't realize the importance of meeting the parents of our proposed pup, the first time around, much less, learning the medical history of the kennel.

If you want to open a window to the potential medical history and disposition of your new child, meeting the parents knowing their history, and that of the kennel, is a great place to start.

We spent a couple of hours visiting and talking with the Sherwood's about the history of their kennel, breeding stock and litters over twenty-five years, but the best part of the trip turned out to be meeting and spending time with those two beautiful shepherds. They greeted and treated us like long lost relatives, and did everything but climb up in to our laps and go to sleep. That response provided insight in to the mental makeup of our future child.

Having been told their offspring would be available early in May, we could hardly wait.

As we got closer to the date, two additional breeders called to say they would have puppies within a month of our target and asked if we would consider them. We said, "thanks, but no thanks."

As you might have guessed by now, we were anxious to bring a new child into our house.

We'd already identified a trainer, bought toys to replace those we'd given to the local animal shelter and begun making many of the same purchases we'd made eleven years earlier in order to begin our second trip through puppy parenthood.

As the birth date drew closer, we found ourselves anxiously awaiting a call to tell us the litter had come into the world, were doing well and that there were girls among the litter. As it turned out, the answers were yes, yes and yes!

I'll never forget sitting on the grass at the Sherwood's several weeks later, holding those new little guys and gals. Watching them romp and tussle with each other was a real treat. We knew we wanted another girl, but one little boy attached himself to me. I couldn't stop playing and petting him, but Carla made it very clear that that was NOT going to happen.

As we headed for home that afternoon the anticipation was electric. We could hardly wait for the little girl we had chosen to reach nine weeks of age.

Florida has a law that puppies are not to be sold until they have their first shots and are nine weeks old. It's a good law. You don't want to take a pup away from its mother too early. The law protects the pups and helps to insure the new owners that they will receive a happy, healthy child.

Remember the cost of Sabrina? At the time, I thought $250 was a lot of money for a puppy. Well, this time around, we found as we spoke to professional breeders that we could expect to pay between $1,000 and $2,000 for a pet. If we wanted our child obedience or attack trained before being turned over to us, the cost multiplied several times.

This time around, we paid $1,200 and signed an agreement stating that if we decided to show our newest little girl, we could expect to receive a fairly large bill. As we had no desire to travel a show circuit again, we said, 'thank you very much." and signed the agreement." Just as before, this little girl would be loved, spoiled and spend all of her days at home with us.

So, now you know — there's a new little girl in town. She will never replace Sabrina — that is not why we decided on another female German shepherd.

We wanted Tia, that's her name, to grow up in her own way, and on her own schedule. While the transformation from puppy to adult was taking place she would be treated as her own special person.

It didn't take long before we realized that Tia was no Sabrina. Maybe we had set the bar too high where our new little girl was concerned, forgetting just that – that she was a NEW little girl.

Looking back on our first months together, Tia created memories that I would like to forget, but they serve to demonstrate that parenthood — life with a new four legged child, can include some ups and downs. Most important, it taught me an excellent life lesson — don't establish preconceived expectations where a new pet is concerned — live from moment to moment.

Our new girl came to us weighing just thirteen pounds, and in a matter of months the transformation from a ball of fur to a very striking young lady in German shepherd clothing was well underway.

Bringing a new pet into your home when you've recently lost one requires that you not only commit time for nurturing, training, and loving them — it demands that you park your emotions, forget any early expectations you may have, and most important — that you exercise patience with a capital "P."

Based upon the health problems we experienced with Sabrina, this time we purchased pet medical insurance. It's an investment I hope we never have to use, but I'm glad it's available.

There are a number of pet insurance companies listed on the Internet. Some veterinarians have literature for your review as well. Take time to look it over. Discuss medical insurance for your pet with your vet, they deal with these companies ever day and are an excellent source of information.

Compare internet and vet recommended plans and if you are financially able, purchase the one that best suits your budget and level of risk. Remember, if you invest in a medical insurance policy you are doing so with the hope that you will never have to use it.

I will never forget the first visit to our vet, with Tia. Dr. Bivens made it perfectly clear that she thought we were nuts. Upon meeting Tia, her first comment went something like this: "Don't you realize that you guys are eleven years older? Here you are, at your ages, starting all over again with a high-energy puppy."

The first time the trainer we'd chosen met Tia, his response parroted Dr. Bivens, "I could have found you a low-energy German shepherd that was a few years old, one that would have been just right for your lifestyle. A shepherd that would have saved you from what you are about to experience."

If Tia is with us for eleven years, well, you get the picture. Carla and I aren't getting any younger. I will be eighty and she would be seventy. This, of course, assumes that we are fortunate to have her with us that long or, based upon the preceding comments, she doesn't kill us before that.

As it turned out, nothing our vet or first trainer could say was going to cause us to question our decision. Well, not at that time, anyway. Besides, we'd made up our minds — both of us wanted to experience the joy and the unconditional love that comes from bringing a puppy in to your heart and home and slowly but surely bonding with it.

We wanted the opportunity to watch our child blossom — to work with and train her. There is nothing more special than suddenly seeing your pup look up at you — with a smile on his or her face as you walk down the street together. Bonding with your pup is a feeling you have to experience to appreciate!

Our first months with Tia turned out to be everything that our vet and trainer said they would be — times two, or maybe three. She was a handful, and if you could have seen my arms and ankles, well, that's where she did most of her initial teething.

At one point, our new child caused Carla to tell me, "I look at her, and I don't love her. I don't even like her."

My reaction was basically the same. I would be lying if I didn't tell you that there were times when I wanted to pick her up and throw her against a wall. Not that I ever would, but the thought crossed my mind.

I'm telling you this, because sometimes — not always, but sometimes, living with a new pup is not a walk in the park!

Tia was very mouthy, and her energy level was beyond anything we'd ever experienced with Sabrina, even though the breeder felt she would was one of the most submissive pups in the litter.

I had scabs everywhere. Her baby teeth and nails constantly left me with broken skin and open wounds. It wasn't intentional; she was just being a puppy. She had to have something to scratch and teeth on, and I was it. I guess having passed seventy years of age my patience wasn't what it was at fifty-nine!

Finally, I was so fed up, I sat down and sent an e-mail to Glenn and Sue Sherwood telling them what I thought of their "submissive" child. I told them that I was just days away from either sending her back, or taking her to the pound!

You should have heard Sue's response. "It's not my dog, it's you!" She went on, but I see no need to bore you with the truth — the truth hurt!

So, with a smile on my face, we decided to try another trainer — sound familiar?

We were driving down the road one day and saw a lady sitting in a convertible on the side of the road. She had the top down, and we could see a very large German shepherd sitting in the backseat.

As her car was off in the grass, we stopped to offer assistance. She said she was just stopping for a moment. Upon finding that she didn't need help, we began to question her about her very well mannered shepherd and told her about our wild child.

Watching her dog sit perfectly still, reminded us why we wanted to make this parental trip a second time. Granted, our chances of surviving our current attempt at parenthood looked dubious at best. Our little angel was a rambunctious, outrageously energetic whirling dervish, but by the time this stranger finished singing the praises of her trainer, we had to meet him.

Within days, we found ourselves watching a training session with more than twenty dogs, of all sizes and shapes, being worked together without a bark, a growl or an out-and-out fight. How did he do it?

Dennis believed in the use of an electric shock collar to train dogs.

"There is nothing wrong with using a shock collar. The shocks are only intended to get your dogs attention," he said. So, we signed up and began attending classes using the collar. Suddenly, Tia began responding to our every training command. However, when we took the collar off, her response depended upon what our inquisitive child was working on at the time.

I didn't like the shock collar from the start, but I couldn't knock its success. I guess it was the Casper-milk-toast father in me rising to the surface. It may not have hurt Tia, but it was hurting me every time I hit the button on the control. I guess I was beginning to fall in love with my child, and the idea of shocking her every time I gave her a simple command just didn't sit well with me.

If you think I wanted Tia off the collar, you should have heard Sue and Glenn the first time we brought Tia up to board for a few days — and they were right!

Don't read into this, that Tia was stupid — just the opposite. With the collar on, she was the fastest learner I have ever seen — although my experience is somewhat limited.

As Tia grew out of the "terrible one's" — year that is — she was beginning to turn into the most lovable clown on four legs. Her initial greeting when confronted with new people was guarded, but given a couple of minutes to sniff and look them over, once approved, all they had to do was remember her name and like another pup we knew and loved, she would give you the keys to the car as well as her favorite toys.

We finally decided to look for a trainer of German shepherds and being unable to find one, I called the Sherwood's and asked Sue if any of her fellow breeders could recommend one.

This led to a search requiring several e-mails and phone calls, but finally, we found Kate Lamont.

We talked with Kate several times. Because one of her dogs was sick, it took us a few months, but we were finally able to take Tia to be evaluated. Kate had a large fenced area behind her house — an area set up to train for protection as well as obedience.

Kate wasn't the evil stepsister of Sergeant Debbie. She was calm and gentle, but with a strong right arm. The next thing we knew, Tia was following Kate and taking direction like an old pro. Who says lightning doesn't strike twice? When Kate was finished looking our little girl over, we heard those now infamous words one more time — "she's an energetic puppy isn't she?"

Well, skip ahead several private lessons at her home and a few conducted at ours, and I am able to report to you that Tia is, as I later reported to Sue and Glenn, with hat in hand — the almost always obedient love of my life!

From the day we bought Tia home, I was down on the floor each night telling her to "sleep well and have good doggie dreams. I told her that we loved her, and would always be there for her." As I spoke these words — words that at another time no doubt went in one ear and out the other of an earlier child — I stroked her head and rubbed her ears.

Through thick and thin, as they say, those words have never changed, even though, during a period in time when we were attempting to "bond" their meaning might not have been heartfelt.

Once I closed the door to her kennel, I would climb in to bed, close my eyes and ask God for all the help and patience I could muster

These days, we take Tia back to board with Sue and Glenn whenever we travel. As we approach their house, Tia will sit up, if she has been asleep on the backseat, and start moving and looking. It's as if she knows she is about to see her mom and dad.

When we pull up next to the long brick building that serves as a boarding kennel and open the back door of the car, she is out in an instant, and when Sue and Glenn come out the back door of their house, well, we've stopped trying to hold on to the leash. We simply drop it and watch as she sprints to see and greet them.

Without meaning a word of it, we've told the Sherwood's that we are jealous. Sue laughed and reminded us that she was the one that brought Tia in to the world — cared for, watched over and played with her for her first nine and a half weeks. Who can argue with that logic!

The new little girl in our life isn't little any more. Today, she stands tall and is a young lady that weighs seventy-five pounds.

In case I haven't mentioned it, allow a father to brag. To my mind, Tia is a beautiful creation. She is a perfectly proportioned German shepherd. Her stance, gait and lines are gifts from a heritage of champions.

When I look across the room at her and see her stretched out on the floor, head up and ears erect, I am in awe of God's ability to once again craft such a child! I know that sounds like high praise, but understand, you are listening to someone that believes each German shepherd has been hand crafted — as if from a block of marble!

She's My Gatekeeper

Do you believe in God?

There was a time in my life when, although I believed that God existed, I just wasn't sure that he had time to listen to me. This was troubling, because if I needed him, how would I know if he heard me — how would I know if he answered?

During my time with Sabrina, and now with Tia, all of my questions have been answered. What I am about to relate to you, may be greeted with a degree of doubt, but in my heart, I believe every word.

I began saying good night to Sabrina from the moment we brought her home. Each night I would kneel on the floor in front of her crate and tell her to, "sleep well and to have good doggie dreams — that her new mother and I loved her and that we would always be there for her."

As the first of her medical issues cropped up, I found myself talking directly to God as I told Sabrina good night, I asked him to watch over her. That was all I asked, and in each instance her doctors diagnosed the problem, solved it and gave her back to me.

Before long her minor problems were overshadowed by major issues that required specialists and surgery. Now, I found myself becoming more specific. Sabrina needed help. Her surgeons needed God to guide their hands and repair her damaged body, and most important, I asked God to return her to me for however much time he would allow the two of us to be together. God never let me down!

He had loaned Sabrina to me for an unspecified period of time. I knew there were no warranties when she entered my life. We would be joined together, "in good times and in bad times, until death separated us." During this unspecified period of time, I believed that Sabrina would love me as much as I loved her.

I was confident that she would protect me if necessary, just as I would do everything in my power to see to it that no matter what she needed, no problem would be left unanswered.

As I hope you can tell from our time together, I think you would have to agree that God did his part, Sabrina did hers — and Carla and I — well, we took Sabrina into our hearts and when she needed us, we became the caregivers that enabled her to be a part of our life for nearly eleven years — far longer than anyone dreamt possible.

With both of our parents and several of our favorite cats already in heaven, when God asked for Sabrina to be returned, I began asking her to watch over and look after everyone. I have never stopped telling her good night. From the moment she left us, I continued to tell her to "sleep well, dream of angels and to look after our loved ones, in heaven," because, I knew that she was an angel.

As the last of our special friends departed I asked that she expand her efforts. Four cats became a part of her watch: Tony, Wolfie, Charlie and finally Randy. We loved all of the cats that came into our lives however these four were very special to us.

I never doubted that Sabrina would step up and take on this task after all, she was still my little girl. I knew she would look after and take good care of everyone!

Tia came in to our lives at a time when I was at my lowest low, I simply refused to admit it. Although we had allowed seven months to pass from the time that Sabrina departed, try as I might, I could not seem to shake the anger within me during our first months together. In retrospect, it is highly possible that unknowingly, I took some of that anger out on Tia.

I knew that puppies came with teeth and it didn't take long before my body reflected Tia's desire to chew — on me. She never bit down hard, but always managed to break the skin. Little by little I lost sight of the fact that she was a puppy.

I never physically abused her during those early months, and I can only hope that she never sensed the anger inside me as I worked to overcome my frustration. The scabs healed, and as they did, they left little red scars, evidence that puppies grow up and love heals all wounds, even the mental ones that no one can see!

Once again, I found myself reaching out to Sabrina. She knew Tia had joined us. Knew that nothing could replace the memories, the love and the bond she and I had forged, as I asked for her help. There had to be a way for her to watch over and help us to mentor our new little girl.

I know this sounds strange, none the less, I asked that if it was God's will, she be allowed to watch over and pass some of her many qualities on to Tia.

I didn't want Tia to become a clone of Sabrina, but if there was some way to guide her through the puppy process and on to becoming a young lady, I would be forever grateful for her help.

My nightly prayers must have been heard because as time passed, Tia began to change. There was no overnight correction. Oh no, it took months, but change she did. She began to settle down — began to respond to Carla and me in all kinds of positive ways.

Suddenly, when her mouth opened, a tongue came out and we were showered with kisses. She was becoming a love machine, and I was in canine heaven!

Need more signs that someone was listening to my ever lengthening goodnight prayer?

All of a sudden, Tia was front and center whenever the ice cube maker was dropping cubes — she had to have hers.

Then the "veggie queen" returned as Tia began to devour carrots, sweet potatoes, Brussels sprouts, peppers and more.

She put on several shows a night with her squeaky toys. She would dance, prance and demand attention, no matter what we were doing, or who was visiting.

I guess Sabrina saved the best for last. I will never forget the first time Tia heard a popcorn popper. She was in the kitchen in an instant, and from that day forward - became a popcorn junky. Suddenly, we could throw popped kernels, ice cubes and veggies for her to catch 'til our arms fell numb. She didn't do it with Sabrina's flair, but then, she's well on her way to becoming her own young lady, with her own flair for acting the entertainer!

Hardly a night goes by that I don't ask Sabrina to watch over everyone and I do mean everyone.

Remember Sabrina and the cats? No matter how we tried, we could never get them to love much less look at each other without the cats hiding behind a screen.

Carla use to say that she longed for the day when she was done cleaning and changing litter boxes. When our last cat, Randy, left us, her wish had been granted. However, as with the departure of Sabrina and the introduction of Tia, once again, there was something missing in our house. We didn't have a cat. They may not greet and love you in the same manner as a dog, but we had loved all of them and we were beginning to feel the need to bring another one into our lives. It would have been easy to head straight for the Pound and pick up a kitten, but deep down we knew that wouldn't do.

Tony had been a feline love machine and character from the day he came in to our home. The more we thought about him, the more convinced we became that we had to find an Ocicat breeder and acquire a little girl.

Our friends in Amarillo, Texas were no longer breeding Ocicats, and had no young females left from their years of "showing", so we asked them for breeder recommendations and Carla began the search.

She found a breeder about sixty miles from us, in Naples, Florida. They began swapping e-mails and conversations on the telephone and before you could say "meow," Carla was on the floor with a bevy of little girls, each with a colored ribbon around their neck for identification.

According to Carla, the choice wasn't difficult, one little girl in particular came into her arms and it was love at first sight — make that "purr."

Holly, a.k.a "Hollister," "bb," for "bubble butt," — because that's the way females of her breed are shaped, joined us at the ripe old age of four months.

Once again, I placed a call to Sabrina, "please watch over Tia and Holly. Instill in them the true meaning of friendship and love for one another," was added to my nightly prayer. If you get the impression that it takes me more than a few minutes to say goodnight to everyone, you're right, but as my requests were being answered — this was no time to stop!

Rome wasn't built in a day, and neither was the friendship between Tia and Holly. It took five months of nightly requests and some outside help, but I am pleased to report that Tia and Holly are now best buddies.

When our efforts to bring the two together failed, we called Kate Lamont to see if she could help. She came over on several occasions to work with Tia, Holly and Carla. They worked together and as they did, Kate provided us with a course of action that we could follow. Little by little the barriers between our children fell away.

Where once, Tia could be seen ready for launch the moment Holly was put on the floor — times have changed. Now, Tia follows Holly wherever she goes and when Tia turns to go in the opposite direction, Holly is not far behind. Tia loves Holly's toys and Holly finds Tia's furry bed full of toys a great place to browse and catch forty winks.

They may look like Mutt and Jeff when they are together, Tia weighs seventy-five-pounds and Holly only seven pounds, yet the love these two share and the pleasure they provide Carla and me as we watch them together is priceless!

Want a Kodak moment? Try this. Tia is stretched out on the floor and Holly is in a similar position resting in-between Tia's front legs as the two of them take a snooze. They're just fine as long as they think we're not watching. Look their way, and one or both will get up and move a few feet.

Sometimes I think they just don't want us to know how much they love each other. Thank you God, and thank you Sabrina, you are always in my prayers.

Is everything I am relating a miracle, or is divine intervention from a very close friend, alive and well?

I don't know, but I do believe that God is listening? He may not respond immediately, but respond he does and no one will ever tell me different!

I seldom if ever ask for anything for myself. However, to this day and for as long as I am alive to do so, I will continue to ask Sabrina to watch over our parents, our cats and Tia and Holly each night when I go to bed.

If you have a pet, or you are thinking about acquiring one, I hope that by now you know the difference between love and unconditional love. If not, allow me.

Love is easy. People fall in and out of it every day.

Unconditional love is a whole 'nother story. It is a two-way street, a shared experience. It is two people — two beings willing to work together and do for each other — without reservation. It is a very special feeling and you will know it when you feel and see it!

Sure, most of us love our pets. After all, they ask so little and they NEVER stop giving. When you find yourself responding in kind, no matter the time, place or reason, well, that's unconditional love.

God made this abundantly clear when he loaned Sabrina to me, and then designated her, MY gatekeeper!

FYI

As you have no doubt gathered, we've been blessed where veterinarians are concerned.

To each of them — Drs. Bivens, Ward, Barnes, and Oakes — I say "thank you." Each of you bring grace and caring to your profession and have always been there for us.

To those of you with pets, I strongly suggest that when selecting a veterinarian you not be afraid to change doctors if you feel your pet is being treated as a number with a prescription attached.

This may require you to try several vets, but I can tell you from experience that you will know when you've found the right one.

And if, at some time, you are faced with a pet medical problem, don't be upset if your vet says, "I don't know, or I'm not sure what is causing the problem." Be glad that you've found a vet that knows enough to know when he or she just doesn't know enough.

When your pet is facing a major problem, don't hesitate to seek a second opinion or to ask, "Where can I find the best course of treatment?"

Surprisingly, for the size of the profession there are too few specialists, but they're out there — you just have to be willing to ask who and where.

Each year millions of pet owners lose their special friends — pets that provided so much joy and asked so little in return.

When we lost Sabrina we grieved. Not for hours or days, but for weeks and months. Even now one or both of us will recall something Sabrina did, and we'll get all teary eyed.

Months after she was gone, we'd start the day with a smile and suddenly, for whatever reason, find ourselves bawling like babies.

We mentioned our experience with the Iams Pet Loss Support Center to Carla's sister. She's a vet in Memphis, Tennessee, and a very good one. She'd never heard of the Support Center, but within a few weeks she was back on the phone with us asking for the number. One of her clients was having a difficult time with her loss and she wanted to put her in touch with one of Iams grief counselors.

We've never asked, but I wouldn't be surprised to find that she's given the number, 1-888-332-7738, out several times.

There are other sources of help. Many can be found by surfing the Internet. Pet grievance assistance can often be found in neighborhood church groups. The idea is new, but they are beginning to spring up around the country.

Some of the aids we found on the internet included: Chance's Spot Pet Loss and Grief Resources, a number of help lines and universities. There were also articles and publications that may help you to better understand your feelings and help you to get through the rough times.

Whatever you do, however you handle your loss, don't be ashamed to grieve. After all - you're only human!

For those of you that may be just starting out with a new puppy, *The Art of Raising a Puppy* by the Monks of New Skete in upstate New York helped us to house and crate train both Sabrina and now Tia. It was such a simple routine, but, oh, how it made life easier for us once we returned to their advice. Before we knew it, both Sabrina and Tia responded the same way.

Today Tia's crate, sits directly across from our bed. It serves as her special place when we are at home, traveling or she just wants some quiet time alone. The door to her crate is always open.

Over the years we've come to believe that our pets need some time each day to themselves. So mid morning and mid afternoon Tia is crated and Holly is sent to her room for a few hours.

If you are reading this book before acquiring a puppy or a dog with a little time under his or her paws know that there is more than one way to acquire your new friend. Breeders, pet stores, animal shelters, breed specialists that take back pups and adults that their owners can no longer afford and even dog tracks that no longer have use for their greyhounds are all places to consider.

If you think you want a pup with a pedigree, don't just look for an individual that claims to be a breeder. Take the time to contact and talk to members of the Breed Association. Find out if there is a professional breeder in your area. Visit a breed show if you have the time. Meet and talk with several breeders. You'll find that most of them love to talk about and show off their children.

These are folks that love what they are doing, and most important, they love and take pride in raising and placing wonderful puppies and on rare occasion, older dogs, in good homes. What they are not — are puppy mills!

A certificate with AKC at the top is no guarantee that the skill and history of the seller — and the quality of the puppy — meet the highest standards. Check them both out before you buy.

Life is a learning experience, and where puppies are concerned love and patience is a recipe for success. If you find yourself experiencing a trip with your new family member similar to ours with Tia, don't give up, count to ten; then repeat the count. Take it from me, it's worth the effort and when you look in the mirror you may find the problem right in front of you.

Make no mistake, I'm no expert — far from it. I'm just someone that found a dog in his carport one day and before he knew it needed to have a dog of his own.

You can't put a price tag on the love and pure pleasure these children of God lavish upon us as they learn and grow.

They ask so little and give so much. Makes you wonder why they leave us so soon, but then, God has a plan for all of us!